# SEC 376 BAIL MATTERS- SUPREME COURT'S LEADING CASE LAWS

## CASE NOTES- FACTS- FINDINGS OF APEX COURT JUDGES & CITATIONS

JAYPRAKASH BANSILAL SOMANI

Dedicated

To

All the Past & Present Judges of the Supreme Court of India.

Salute to their wisdom.

Salute to their interpretation of Law.

Salute to their elaborative judgement writing.

🙏🙏🙏

# Contents



"

# Preface

**Dear Learned Advocates of the Trial Courts, Session Courts, High Courts, Supreme Court & Individuals,**

I am very delighted to provide you a book on 'SEC 376 ACT BAIL MATTERS'-Supreme Court of India Leading Case Laws.

In this book you will get...

**1.** Name of the Case i. e. Cause title

**2.**Relevant Sections discussed in the case

**3.** Hon'ble Judges/Coram of the case

**4.**Number of PDF Pages in Original Judgement of the case

**5.** All available Citations of the case

**6.** Case Note with appeal allowed/ dismissed or disposed off

**7.** Facts of the case

**8.** Hon'ble Apex Court's findings, while dismissing/allowing or disposing the appeal

**9.** Ratio Decidendi if any.

My special thanks to Manupatra, because of their web portal I can compile this book in well manner. I am also thankful to Notion Press to support me to publish & market this book throughout the Country. Thanks to my Juniors, Advocate Colleagues & Insolvency Professional Colleagues to support me in this venture.

**Miss Shruti Kriti** has helped me a lot to compile this book.

I hope this book will add some value addition in the wealth of your legal knowledge. Your positive feedbacks will boost me to compile/ write further books & negative feedbacks will improve my skills. Kindly send your valuable feedbacks by email.

Thanks with Regards,

**Jayprakash B. Somani**

Advocate, Supreme Court of India

**Email:** jaysomani64@gmail.com

**Web Site:**www.jayprakashsomani.com

**Call:** 9322188701, 8459194576

ᐅᐅᐅ

# Acknowledgements

**Acknowledgement**
**Printed & Published by**
**Notion Press**
No. 8, 3$^{rd}$ Cross Street,
CIT Colony, Mylapore,
Chennai, Tamil Nadu- 600004

ᐅᐅᐅ

**Managed by**
**Jayprakash Somani Advocates & Solicitors**
**Law Firm for Supreme Court of India**
**Delhi Office**
B-851, 1$^{st}$ Floor, Shivaji Marg (Charch Wali Gali),
New Ashok Nagar, Delhi 110096
Call 9322188701, 8459194576
**Supreme Court Chamber**
312, 3$^{rd}$ Floor, M. C. Setalvad Block, In front of 'D' Gate, Bhagwan Das
Road, Supreme Court of India, New Delhi 110001
Contact: 8459194576, 9811011747
**www.jayprakashsomani.com**

ᐅᐅᐅ

**Books are available online in India**
**1. Notion Press:**https://notionpress.com/author/jayprakash_somani
**2. Amazon:**https://www.amazon.in/s?k=jayprakash+somani
**3. Flipkart:**https://www.flipkart.com/search?q=Jayprakash%20Somani
**Books are available online at International Market**
**4.     Amazon     International:**     https://www.amazon.com/
s?k=jayprakash+somani
**5.     Amazon     United     Kingdom:**     https://www.amazon.co.uk/
s?k=jayprakash+somani
**6. E-Books/Kindle edition at National & International Level:**
https://www.amazon.in/s?k=jaypraksh+somani

ᐅᐅᐅ

# ONE

# P Vs. The State of Madhya Pradesh and Ors., 2022

**Hon'ble Judges/Coram**: N.V. Ramana, C.J.I., Krishna Murari and Hima Kohli, JJ.

**Act/ Sections**:Code of Criminal Procedure, 1973 (CrPC) - Section 161, Code of Criminal Procedure, 1973 (CrPC) - Section 164, Code of Criminal Procedure, 1973 (CrPC) - Section 437(1), Code of Criminal Procedure, 1973 (CrPC) - Section 438, Code of Criminal Procedure, 1973 (CrPC) - Section 439, Code of Criminal Procedure, 1973 (CrPC) - Section 439(1); Indian Penal Code, 1860 (IPC) - Section 34, Indian Penal Code, 1860 (IPC) - Section 143, Indian Penal Code, 1860 (IPC) - Section 188, Indian Penal Code, 1860 (IPC) - Section 294, Indian Penal Code, 1860 (IPC) - Section 323, Indian Penal Code, 1860 (IPC) - Section 324, Indian Penal Code, 1860 (IPC) - Section 376(2), Indian Penal Code, 1860 (IPC) - Section 452, Indian Penal Code, 1860 (IPC) - Section 506

**No. of pages of the original Judgement**: 11

**Citation**: AIR2022SC2183, MANU/SC/0587/2022

**Case Note**: Criminal - Cancellation of Bail - Scope of powers of Court - Section 439 of the Code of Criminal Procedure, 1973 - Offences allegedly committed under Sections 376(2)(n) and 506 of the Indian Penal Code, 1860 (IPC) - Whether High Court overlooked criminal antecedents and also ignoring material evidence while granting bail to Respondent No. 2?

**Facts**: The present appeal questioned the order allowing application filed by Respondent No. 2/Accused whereby granting bail in connection with case registered on the complaint of Appellant for the offences punishable under Sections 376(2)(n) and 506 of the Indian Penal Code, 1860. Respondent No. 2 alleged to have induced Appellant/complainant to establish a physical relationship with him on the false pretext of marrying her. When the Appellant informed Respondent No. 2 that she was pregnant, he along with his sister had taken her to a private hospital and made her undergo abortion, without her knowledge. As further alleged, the Respondent No. 2 refused to solemnize marriage. Impugned order granted Respondent No. 2 regular bail. Hence the present appeal.

**Hon'ble Apex Court Held, while allowing the Appeal:** High Court or for that matter, the Sessions Court have a wide discretion in deciding an application for bail under Section 439 Code of Criminal Procedure However, the said discretion must be exercised after due application of the judicial mind and not in a routine manner.

For cancelling bail once granted, the Court must consider whether any supervening circumstances have arisen or the conduct of the Accused post grant of bail demonstrates that it is no longer conducive to a fair trial to permit him to retain his freedom by enjoying the concession of bail during trial.

A perusal of the impugned order goes to show that the sole ground on which the concession of bail has been extended by the High Court to the Respondent No. 2 is the delay on the part of the Appellant/complainant in lodging the FIR, without offering any plausible explanation for the same. Absence of cogent reasons and failure to refer to the relevant factors that weighed with the Court to grant bail is also an important factor that can persuade the Appellate Court to interfere with the order passed.

The impugned order reveals that the High Court has made short shrift of the submissions made by the prosecution counsel to the effect that in her statements recorded under Sections 161 and 164 Code of Criminal Procedure, the Appellant/complainant has not waivered and stuck to her version and the fact that the Respondent No. 2 has previous criminal history. It is worthwhile to note that the criminal antecedents of the Respondent No. 2 were brought to the notice of the High Court by the Appellant/complainant and learned Counsel for the Respondent No. 1/State has also confirmed that he is involved in at least four criminal cases.

Respondent No. 2 does not deserve the concession of bail. Relevant material brought on record has been overlooked by the High Court while granting him bail. Accordingly, the impugned order is quashed and set aside and the Respondent No. 2 is directed to surrender.

**Appeal allowed.**

# TWO

# BHADRESH BIPINBHAI SHETH VS. STATE OF GUJARAT AND ORS., 2015

**Hon'ble Judges/Coram:** A.K. Sikri and Rohinton Fali Nariman, JJ.

**Act/ Sections:** Indian Penal Code, 1860 (IPC) - Section 34, Indian Penal Code, 1860 (IPC) - Section 149, Indian Penal Code, 1860 (IPC) - Section 376, Indian Penal Code, 1860 (IPC) - Section 506(2); Code of Criminal Procedure, 1973 (CrPC) - Section 46, Code of Criminal Procedure, 1973 (CrPC) - Section 173(8), Code of Criminal Procedure, 1973 (CrPC) - Section 437, Code of Criminal Procedure, 1973 (CrPC) - Section 438, Code of Criminal Procedure, 1973 (CrPC) - Section 438(1), Code of Criminal Procedure, 1973 (CrPC) - Section 439, Code of Criminal Procedure, 1973 (CrPC) - Section 498; Constitution of India - Article 21

**No. of pages of the original Judgement:**12

**Citation:** AIR2015SC3090, (2016)1SCC152, MANU/SC/0949/2015

**Case Note:** Criminal - Anticipatory bail - Section 438 Code of Criminal Procedure, 1973 and Section 376 Indian Penal Code, 1860 - Prosecutrix filed complaint against Appellant making various allegations - Proceedings began in 2001 - Prosecutrix made application for addition of alleged rape in complaint in 2010 - Appellant granted anticipatory bail by trial court - Set aside by High Court on Prosecutrix's appeal - Whether the High Court erred in setting aside the order of the trial court granting anticipatory bail to the

Appellant.

**Facts:** The Appellant and the Prosecutrix were neighbours and known to each other. On 29.05.2001, the Prosecutrix wrote a complaint to the police commissioner alleging harassment by the Appellant meted out over a period of time. Allegations of rape, emotional blackmail and threats were levelled against the Appellant. On 31.05.2001, her statement was recorded by a police officer where she again levelled the allegations of maltreatment, blackmail and more, however, in this statement recorded by the Investigating Officer, allegations of rape were not made. In 2010, the Prosecutrix made an application for addition of charge under Section 376 IPC as well. On 31.03.2012, the magistrate directed the police to carry out special investigation. Subsequently, the Police filed a revised chargesheet stating that a prima facie case Under Section 376 IPC was also made out. In view of addition of charge under Section 376 IPC, the magistrate passed the order on 25.04.2013 for committal of proceedings to the Sessions Court and taking the Appellant into custody. However, execution of this order for taking the Appellant into custody was stayed till 07.05.2013. The Appellant moved the Sessions Court for grant of anticipatory bail which was ultimately granted on 18.05.2013. The Prosecutrix filed criminal petition before the High Court, which was allowed, cancelling the anticipatory bail granted to the Appellant. Hence, the present appeal.

**Hon'ble Apex Court Held, allowing the appeal:** 1. In the case of Gurbaksh Singh Sibbia and Ors. v. State of Punjab it was emphasized that provision of anticipatory bail in Section 438 IPC are conceptualised under Article 21 of the Constitution. Thus, liberal interpretation of Section 438 IPC must be made. Further relying on the principle laid down in Siddharam Satlingappa Mhetre v. State of Maharashtra and Ors, no purpose would be served in refusing anticipatory bail to the Appellant in respect of alleged incident which is 17 years old and for which the charge is framed only in the year 2014. The investigation is complete and there is no allegation that the Appellant may flee the course of justice. The Appellant has participated in proceedings ongoing since 2001. There is no allegation that during this period he had tried to influence the witnesses. Thus, even when there is a serious charge levelled against the Appellant, that by itself is not reason to deny anticipatory bail when the matter is examined keeping in view other factors.

2. The Prosecutrix has moved an application in these proceedings for perusing new evidence on the basis of which she claims that the Appellant has committed breach of conditions of anticipatory bail and regular bail. It is not necessary for us to go into the allegations made in this application. She would be at liberty to make such an application before the trial court for cancellation of bail.

ԲԲԲ

# THREE

# SANGITABEN SHAILESHBHAI DATANTA VS. STATE OF GUJARAT, 2018

**Hon'ble Judges/Coram:** N.V. Ramana and Mohan M. Shantanagoudar, JJ.

**Act/ Sections**: Protection of Children From Sexual Offences Act, 2012 - Section 4, Protection of Children From Sexual Offences Act, 2012 - Section 5, Protection of Children From Sexual Offences Act, 2012 - Section 6, Protection of Children From Sexual Offences Act, 2012 - Section 8, Protection of Children From Sexual Offences Act, 2012 - Section 9, Protection of Children From Sexual Offences Act, 2012 - Section 10, Protection of Children From Sexual Offences Act, 2012 - Section 23, Protection of Children From Sexual Offences Act, 2012 - Section 33(7); Indian Penal Code, 1860 (IPC) - Section 228A, Indian Penal Code, 1860 (IPC) - Section 376, Indian Penal Code, 1860 (IPC) - Section 376A, Indian Penal Code, 1860 (IPC) - Section 376AB, Indian Penal Code, 1860 (IPC) - Section 376B, Indian Penal Code, 1860 (IPC) - Section 376C, Indian Penal Code, 1860 (IPC) - Section 376D, Indian Penal Code, 1860 (IPC) - Section 376DA, Indian Penal Code, 1860 (IPC) - Section 376DB, Indian Penal Code, 1860 (IPC) - Section 376E, Indian Penal Code, 1860 (IPC) - Section 376(2); Code of Criminal Procedure, 1973 (CrPC) - Section 439

**No. of pages of the original Judgement**: 04

**Citation:** (2019)14SCC522, MANU/SC/1361/2018

**Case Note:** Criminal - Bail - Validity of grant - Sections 376(2)(f) and 376(2)(i) of Indian Penal Code, 1860; Sections 4, 5(c)(f)(m), 6, 8, 9(c)(f)(m),10, 23 and 33(7) of Protection of Children from Sexual Offences Act, 2012 - FIR was lodged against Respondent No. 2 under Sections 376(2)(f) and 376(2)(i) of Code and Sections 4, 5(c)(f)(m), 6, 8, 9(c)(f)(m) and 10 of Act by Appellant - Respondent No. 2 was apprehended thereafter and Charge-Sheet was filed for offence mentioned in FIR - Respondent No. 2 approached High Court for bail and same was granted - Hence, present appeal - Whether High Court erred in granting bail to Respondent No.2.

**Facts:** An FIR was lodged against Respondent No. 2 under Sections 376(2)(f) and 376(2)(i) of the Indian Penal Code and Sections 4, 5(c)(f)(m), 6, 8, 9(c)(f)(m) and 10 of the POCSO Act, by the Appellant, who was grandmother of the victim. Respondent No. 2 was apprehended thereafter and Charge-Sheet was filed for the offence mentioned in the FIR. Therein, Respondent No. 2 approached the High Court for bail and the same was granted.

**Hon'ble Apex Court Held, while allowing the appeal:** (i) In the instant case, by ordering the scientific tests viz., lie detector, brain mapping and Narco-Analysis and venturing into the reports of the same with meticulous details, the High Court had converted the adjudication of a bail matter to that of a mini-trial indeed. This assumption of function of a trial court by the High Court was deprecated.

(ii) The concern of the legislature in protecting the identity of the victim was further evident from the provisions of POCSO Act. Section 33(7) of the same casts a duty on the Special Court to ensure that identity of the victim is not disclosed at any time during the course of investigation or trial. Further, Section 23 of POCSO Act provides restriction on any form of media to disclose the identity of the victim which tends to lower her reputation or infringes upon her privacy. No disclosure of any particulars is allowed which can eventually lead to disclosure of the identity of the victim.

(iii) Thus, taking note of the violation of settled principles of criminal law jurisprudence and statutory prescriptions vis-C -vis conversion of adjudication of bail application to a mini-trial and disclosure of identity of the victim by the High Court, this Court disapproves the manner in which the High Court had adjudicated the bail application and accordingly, quash the order passed by the High Court.

# FOUR

# STATE OF U.P. VS. GAYATRI PRASAD PRAJAPATI, 2020

**Hon'ble Judges/Coram:** Ashok Bhushan, R. Subhash Reddy and M.R. Shah, JJ.

**Act/ Sections:** Indian Penal Code, 1860 (IPC) - Section 376, Indian Penal Code, 1860 (IPC) - Section 376(D), Indian Penal Code, 1860 (IPC) - Section 504, Indian Penal Code, 1860 (IPC) - Section 506, Indian Penal Code, 1860 (IPC) - Section 511; Protection of Children from Sexual Offences Act, 2012 - Section 3, Protection of Children from Sexual Offences Act, 2012 - Section 4

**No. of pages of the original Judgement: 06**

**Citation:** AIR2020SC5014, MANU/SC/0765/2020

**Case Note**: Criminal - Interim Bail - Medical Grounds - Allowed during the pendency of main application - Offence allegedly committed under 376(D)/376/511/504/506 of Indian Penal Code, 1860 (IPC) read with Sections 3/4 of POCSO Act - Two prior bail applications by Respondent were already dismissed - During the pendency of third application, interim bail was sought on medical grounds - High Court directed medical tests and later granted interim bail - Whether the interim bail as granted was correct? - State aggrieved by impugned order in appeal

**Facts:** The Respondent, a former minister in the State of U.P., is accused in case under Sections 376(D)/376/511/504/506 of Indian Penal Code read with Sections 3/4 of POCSO Act. The Respondent was granted bail by the Sessions

Court which was cancelled before the Respondent could be released from the jail by the High Court on an application filed by the State of U.P. Another Bail Application filed by the Respondent was again rejected by the High Court. The Respondent was admitted for treatment in the hospital. He moved a Bail Application No. 5743 of 2019 before the High Court followed by an application seeking interim bail on medical grounds for a period of six months. The High Court by impugned order allowed the interim bail application on medical grounds. Hence, the State aggrieved by the order in present appeal.

**Hon'ble Apex Court Held, while allowing the Appeal**: The reports of hospital and the medical board, which was brought in the notice of the High Court were neither considered nor referred to by the High Court in the impugned order. When the Respondent was being given treatment in the super-speciality hospital there were no shortcomings in the medical treatment offered to Respondent, which could have been the basis for grant of interim bail on medical ground. Further, as per condition (ii) mentioned in paragraph 27, the High Court contemplated that Respondent shall ordinarily reside at a place of residence, as assured, far from the place of residence of the prosecutrix and her immediate family, thus, the contemplation was that Respondent shall reside at his residence. There was no satisfaction recorded by the High Court that treatment offered to Respondent was not adequate and he requires any further treatment by any particular medical institute for which it is necessary to release the Respondent on interim bail on medical grounds.

Even as on date, due medical care is being taken of the Respondent, which is apparent from the additional documents filed along with the application. The High Court, without considering the entire materials on record, has passed the impugned order which is unsustainable.

In result, appeal allowed with a clarification that observations made are only for deciding the present appeal and shall have no bearing on the merits of the Bail Application, pending before the High Court for consideration.

ᐅᐅᐅ

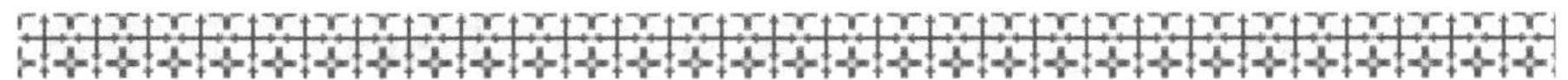

# FIVE

# Union of India (UOI) and Ors. Vs. Dharam Pal, 2019

**Hon'ble Judges/Coram**: N.V. Ramana, Mohan M. Shantanagoudar and S. Abdul Nazeer, JJ.

**Act/ Sections**: Prisoners Act, 1894 - Section 30, Prisoners Act, 1894 - Section 30(2); Indian Penal Code, 1860 (IPC) - Section 34, Indian Penal Code, 1860 (IPC) - Section 73, Indian Penal Code, 1860 (IPC) - Section 74, Indian Penal Code, 1860 (IPC) - Section 302, Indian Penal Code, 1860 (IPC) - Section 376, Indian Penal Code, 1860 (IPC) - Section 452; Constitution of India - Article 21; Constitution of India - Article 32, Constitution of India - Article 72, Constitution of India - Article 161

**No. of pages of the Original Judgement: 08**

**Citation:** (2019)15SCC388, MANU/SC/0627/2019

**Case Note:** Criminal - Death penalty - Section 302/34 of Indian Penal Code, 1860 (IPC) and Section 30 of the Prisoners Act, 1894 - Instant appeal was directed by State against decision of High Court whereby the High Court allowed Writ Petition filed by Respondent Dharam Pal, and commuted death sentence awarded to him to life imprisonment - Respondent was tried and convicted under Section 302/34 of IPC for the commission of murder of five persons belonging to the same family - Whether High Court had erred in setting aside sentence of death of Respondent and commuting same into life imprisonment

**Facts:** Respondent Dharam Pal, in an earlier incident, was convicted under Section 376/452 of IPC vide judgment passed by the Additional Sessions Judge, and sentenced to undergo rigorous imprisonment for ten years. The Respondent was released on bail by the High Court while admitting his appeal, however on the intervening night, Respondent accompanied by his brother Nirmal Singh committed the murder of five persons who were the family members of the prosecutrix for whose rape the Respondent was convicted. The Respondent and his brother were tried and convicted under Section 302/34 of the IPC by the Sessions Court, vide its judgment, the said Court sentenced both the Accused to be hanged until death. Death Reference was heard and the conviction and sentence was affirmed by the High Court by its judgment. The Respondent and his brother, further filed an appeal before this Court, which came to be partly allowed, commuting the death sentence of the Respondent's brother Nirmal Singh into life imprisonment, but upheld the death sentence of the Respondent taking into account his conviction in the rape case, and commission of murder of five family members of the prosecutrix of that case while on bail. Respondent filed the impugned Writ Petition before the High Court praying for his death sentence to be commuted to life imprisonment in light of the change in circumstances viz. his acquittal in the rape case, which was an important deciding factor by this Court in negating his appeal. He also challenged it on grounds of delay in deciding his mercy petition by the President, among other grounds. The High Court while allowing his Writ Petition held that it is a case of violation of the fundamental rights of the Respondent, which makes him eligible for getting his death sentence commuted to life imprisonment, and orders were passed accordingly. The State has filed this appeal against the decision of the High Court.

**Hon'ble Apex Court Held, while disposing of the appeal:** 1. It is admitted that, the Respondent has undergone incarceration for a total period of over 25 years, out of which 18 years were in solitary confinement. Throughout the period of deciding his mercy petition by the President, he was kept in solitary confinement in various jails. Solitary confinement prior to the disposal of the mercy petition is per se illegal and amounts to separate and additional punishment not authorized by law. Section 30 of Act, 1894 provides that, every prisoner under sentence of death shall, immediately on his arrival in the prison after sentence, be searched by, or by order of, the Jailer and all articles shall be taken from him which the Jailer deems it dangerous or inexpedient to leave in his possession. Every such prisoner shall be confined in a cell apart from all other prisoners, and shall be placed by day and by night under the charge of a guard.

2. Thus, solitary confinement prior to the rejection of mercy petition, which has taken place in spite of various decisions of this Court to the contrary, is unfortunate and palpably illegal. In the present case, the Respondent underwent such a long period of solitary confinement that too, prior to his mercy petition being rejected, thereby making it a formidable case for commuting his death sentence into life imprisonment, as rightly held by the High Court.

3. High Court examined the inordinate delay in disposing the mercy petition in the right perspective to hold it illegal, and thereafter commuted the sentence to life imprisonment in light of principles of law laid down in Shatrughan Chauhan. These aspects, coupled with the fact that the authorities did not place the records regarding the acquittal of the Respondent in the rape case before the President for consideration of the mercy petition has caused grave injustice and prejudice against the Respondent. On receipt of a mercy petition, the Department concerned has to call for all the records and materials connected with the conviction. When the matter is placed before the President, it is incumbent on the part of the concerned authority to place all the materials such as judgments of the courts, as well as any other relevant material connected with the conviction. In the present case, this Court while upholding the death sentence of the Respondent and commuting the sentence of his brother to life imprisonment had placed reliance on the fact that the Respondent was convicted in the rape case, and the persons who he had killed were the family members of the prosecutrix of the rape case. The fact that he was subsequently acquitted for that case has great bearing on the quantum on sentence that ought to be awarded to the Respondent and the same should have been brought to the notice of the President while deciding his mercy petition. Failure to do so has caused irreparable prejudice against the Respondent.

4. High Court has not erred in setting aside the sentence of death of the Respondent and commuting the same into life imprisonment. In view of reasons discussed and unconscionable delay of more than 13 years in deciding the mercy petition, the failure to produce the relevant documents regarding the Respondent before the President for deciding the mercy petition, and that the Respondent has undergone 18 years of illegal solitary

confinement, there is no reason to interfere with the decision of the High Court. However, considering the fact that the Respondent had violated the conditions of bail imposed on him by the High Court in criminal appeal, as he had committed the murder of five persons while on bail, cannot be overlooked while quantifying the actual sentence. It would be appropriate to direct the release of the Respondent after the completion of 35 years of actual imprisonment including the period already undergone by him.

5. Appeal disposed off.

ppp

# SIX

# X Vs. The State of Telangana and Ors., 2018

**Hon'ble Judges/Coram**: Dipak Misra, C.J.I., A.M. Khanwilkar and Dr. D.Y. Chandrachud, JJ.

**Act/ Sections:** Indian Penal Code, 1860 (IPC) - Section 342, Indian Penal Code, 1860 (IPC) - Section 354(C), Indian Penal Code, 1860 (IPC) - Section 376, Indian Penal Code, 1860 (IPC) - Section 493, Indian Penal Code, 1860 (IPC) - Section 506; Code of Criminal Procedure, 1973 (CrPC) - Section 439

**No. of pages of the Original Judgement**: 07

**Citation:** AIR2018SC2466, (2018)16SCC511, MANU/SC/0583/2018

**Case Note:** Criminal - Cancellation of bail - Denial of - Sections 439 of Code of Criminal Procedure, 1973 and Sections 342,354(C),376,493 and 506 of Indian Penal Code, 1860 - Charge-sheet had been submitted against accused for offences punishable under Sections 376, 342, 493, 506 and 354 (C) of Code - Accused was granted anticipatory bail which was cancelled by Sessions Judge, principally on ground that Accused had not disclosed fact that he had been Accused in another case - Order of cancellation was affirmed by High Court and by this Court - Accused then moved application under Section 439 of Code for the grant of bail - High Court had allowed application for grant of bail - Hence, present appeal - Whether impugned order of grant of bail warrant any interference.

**Facts:** The complainant alleged that the Accused had been making false promises of marriage to her and was exploiting her continuously. A complaint was lodged and after investigation, a charge-sheet had been submitted for offences punishable under Sections 376, 342, 493, 506 and 354 (C) of the Penal Code. The Accused was granted anticipatory bail by the Fourth Additional Metropolitan Sessions Judge. The order of anticipatory bail was cancelled by the Sessions Judge, principally on the ground that the Accused had not disclosed the fact that he had been Accused in the 2G Spectrum case. The order of cancellation was affirmed by the High Court and by this Court. The Accused then moved an application under Section 439 for the grant of bail. The High Court had allowed the application for the grant of bail and had directed that the Accused be released on executing a personal bond with two sureties each in a like sum to the satisfaction of the Metropolitan Magistrate.

**Hon'ble Apex Court Held, while dismissing the appeal:** (i) The Accused had the benefit of an order granting him anticipatory bail. The grant of anticipatory bail was cancelled principally on the ground that he had not disclosed the pendency of a prosecution against him in the 2G Spectrum case. The Court had been informed during the course of the hearing that the said prosecution had ended in an acquittal. Regular bail was granted by the High Court in the present case. The second FIR which was lodged was not, a supervening circumstance of such a nature as would warrant the cancellation of the bail which was granted by the High Court. The Accused had submitted that the lodging of the second FIR, four days after the order of bail was merely an attempt to bolster a case based on a supervening event and that it suffers from vagueness and a complete absence of details.

(ii) The order of the High Court allowing the application for bail could not be faulted. Moreover, no supervening circumstance had been made out to warrant the cancellation of the bail. There was no cogent material to indicate that the Accused had been guilty of conduct which would warrant his being deprived of his liberty.

ppp

# SEVEN

## SHAMSHER SINGH VERMA VS. STATE OF HARYANA, 2015

**Hon'ble Judges/Coram:** Dipak Misra and Prafulla C. Pant, JJ.

**Act/ Sections:** Protection of Children from Sexual Offences Act, 2015 - Section 4, Protection of Children from Sexual Offences Act, 2015 - Section 12; Code of Criminal Procedure, 1973 (CrPC) - Section 294, Code of Criminal Procedure, 1973 (CrPC) - Section 294(1), Code of Criminal Procedure, 1973 (CrPC) - Section 313; Indian Evidence Act, 1872 - Section 3; Indian Penal Code, 1860 (IPC) - Section 354, Indian Penal Code, 1860 (IPC) - Section 354A, Indian Penal Code, 1860 (IPC) - Section 376

**No. of pages of the Original Judgement: 05**

**Citation:** (2016)15SCC485, MANU/SC/1345/2015

**Case Note:** Criminal - Application under Section 294 - Code of Criminal Procedure, 1973 - Report lodged against Appellant - Offence under Section 354 - Indian Penal Code - One relating to Protection of Children from Sexual Offences Act, 2015 - Charge sheet filed against Appellant - Statement of Accused recorded - Section 313 of Code of Criminal Procedure - Accused moved an application Under Section 294 - Code of Criminal Procedure - Rejected by Trial Court - Rejection affirmed by High Court - Present appeal - Whether the lower courts erred in not allowing the application of the Accused to get played the compact disc relating to alleged conversation between victim's father and son and wife of the Appellant regarding alleged property dispute - Whether the accused has been denied the right of defence

**Facts:** A report was lodged against the Appellant (accused) at Police Station in respect of offence punishable under Section 354 of the Indian Penal Code, 1860 (Indian Penal Code) and one relating to Protection of Children from Sexual Offences Act, 2015 (POCSO) in which complainant alleged that his minor niece was molested by the Appellant. After investigation, a charge sheet was filed against the Appellant, on the basis of which Sessions Case was registered. Special Judge, after hearing the parties, framed charge in respect of offences punishable Under Sections 354A and 376 Indian Penal Code and also in respect of offence punishable Under Sections 4/12 of POCSO. Statement of the accused was recorded Under Section 313 of the Code of Criminal Procedure, 1973 (Code of Criminal Procedure).

In defence, the Accused moved an application Under Section 294 Code of Criminal Procedure before the trial court to play the compact disc relating to conversation between father of the victim and son and wife of the Appellant regarding alleged property dispute. The application was opposed by the prosecution. Consequently, the trial court rejected the same. The same was affirmed by High Court. The present appeal is against the said order of the High Court.

**Hon'ble Apex Court Held, while allowing the appeal**: The object of Section 294 Code of Criminal Procedure is to accelerate pace of trial by avoiding the time being wasted by the parties in recording the unnecessary evidence. Where genuineness of any document is admitted, or its formal proof is dispensed with, the same maybe read in evidence.

In view of the definition of 'document' in Evidence Act, and the law laid down by this Court, the Court held that the compact disc is also a document. It is not necessary for the court to obtain admission or denial on a document Under Sub-section (1) to Section 294 Code of Criminal Procedure personally from the accused or complainant or the witness. The endorsement of admission or denial made by the counsel for defence, on the document filed by the prosecution or on the application/report with which same is filed, is sufficient compliance of Section 294 Code of Criminal Procedure. Similarly on a document filed by the defence, endorsement of admission or denial by the public prosecutor is sufficient and defence will have to prove the document if not admitted by the prosecution. In case it is admitted, it need not be formally proved, and can be read in evidence. In a complaint case such an endorsement can be made by the counsel for the complainant in respect of document filed by the defence.

The Court is not inclined to go into the truthfulness of the conversation sought to be proved by the defence but, in the facts and circumstances of the case, as discussed above, the Court was of the view that the courts below have erred in law in not allowing the application of the defence to get played the compact disc relating to conversation between father of the victim and son and wife of the Appellant regarding alleged property dispute. In Court's opinion, the courts below have erred in law in rejecting the application to play the compact disc in question to enable the public prosecutor to admit or deny, and to get it sent to the Forensic Science Laboratory, by the defence. The Appellant is in jail and there appears to be no intention on his part to unnecessarily linger the trial, particularly when the prosecution witnesses have been examined.

Therefore, without expressing any opinion as to the final merits of the case, this appeal is allowed, and the orders passed by the courts below are set aside. The application dated 19.2.2015 shall stand allowed. However, in the facts and circumstances of the case, it is observed that the accused/ Appellant shall not be entitled to seek bail on the ground of delay of trial.

ppp

# EIGHT

# STATE (GOVT. OF NCT OF DELHI) VS. PANKAJ CHAUDHARY AND ORS., 2018

**Hon'ble Judges/Coram: R. Banumathi and Indira Banerjee, JJ.**
  **Act/ Section**: INDIAN PENAL CODE, 1860 (IPC) - Section 376 (2)(g)
  **No. of pages of the Original Judgement: 013**
  **Citation**: AIR2018SC5412, (2019)11SCC575, MANU/SC/1236/2018
  **Case Note**: Criminal - Acquittal - Legality - Section 376(2)(g) of Indian Penal Code, 1860 (IPC) - Present appeals arose out of judgment passed by High Court by which High Court allowed appeal filed by Respondents/ Accused thereby setting aside their conviction under Section 376(2)(g) of IPC passed by the trial Court - Whether order of acquittal passed by High Court and direction to lodge complaint against police officials was liable to be set aside.

  **Facts:** Charges were framed against Accused/Respondents under Section 376(2)(g) of IPC to which they pleaded not guilty. To bring home guilt of Accused, prosecution examined seven witnesses and exhibited number of documents. Accused/Respondents in their statement under Section 313 of Code of Criminal Procedure, 1973 (CrPC) stated that PW-1-Prosecutrix was of bad character and she was indulging in prostitution and they have lodged complaint against her and therefore, they had been falsely implicated in rape case. Trial court convicted Accused/Respondents under Section

376(2)(g) of IPC and sentenced each of them to undergo rigorous imprisonment for ten years. Being aggrieved, Accused/Respondents filed appeal before High Court. High Court by impugned judgment allowed appeal by setting aside conviction. High Court held that, regarding the ladies' quarrel involving sex workers including prosecutrix FIR was registered and in connection with said FIR, prosecutrix and other ladies were arrested and that they were in custody with police. High Court therefore doubted prosecution case and held that when prosecutrix and other ladies were in custody with police during relevant time, it was impossible that, occurrence of rape would have taken place as alleged by prosecutrix.

**Hon'ble Apex Court Held, while allowing the appeal**: as rightly held by trial Court that even if allegations of Accused that, prosecutrix was of immoral character were taken to be correct, same did not give any right to Accused persons to commit rape on her against her consent.

Even in cases where there was some material to show that, victim was habituated to sexual intercourse, no inference like victim being a woman of 'loose moral character" iwa permissible to be drawn from that circumstance alone. A woman of easy virtue also could not be raped by a person for that reason.

Conviction could be sustained on sole testimony of prosecutrix if it inspired confidence.

Trial Court which had opportunity of seeing and observing prosecutrix, found testimony of prosecutrix reliable being corroborated by her mother's evidence, medical evidence, FSL report and other circumstances viz. absence of motive for any false implication etc. While so, High Court ought not to have heavily interfered with verdict of conviction based on alleged time gap in registration of two FIRs and other aspects of investigation in connection with FIR No. 558/97 to reverse verdict of conviction.

While passing disparaging remarks against police officials and directing prosecution against them, High Court had failed to bear in mind well settled principles of law that should govern Courts before making disparaging remarks. Any disparaging remarks and direction to initiate departmental action/prosecution against persons whose conduct comes into consideration before Court would have serious impact on their official career.

It had been consistently held by present Court that, prosecution for perjury be sanctioned by Courts only in those cases where perjury appears to be deliberate and that prosecution ought to be ordered where it would be expedient in interest of justice to punish the delinquent and not merely because there was some inaccuracy in statement.

High Court had not recorded a finding that "it was expedient in interest of justice to initiate an inquiry into offences punishable under Sections 193 and 195 of IPC against police officials and under Section 211 of IPC against the prosecutrix". Without affording an opportunity of hearing to police officials and based on materials produced before appellate Court, High Court was not right in issuing direction to Registrar General to lodge a complaint against police officials and said direction was liable to be set aside.

Even assuming that, prosecutrix was of easy virtue, she had a right of refuse to submit herself to sexual intercourse to anyone. Judgment of High Court reversing verdict of conviction under Section 376(2)(g) recorded by trial Court could not be sustained and is liable to be set aside.

Impugned judgment of High Court was set aside and appeal preferred by State was allowed. Verdict of conviction of Accused-Respondent under Section 376(2)(g) of IPC and also the sentence of imprisonment of ten years imposed upon them was affirmed. Direction of High Court to lodge complaint against police officials was set aside.

Appeal allowed.

ppp

# NINE

# YOGESH AND ORS. VS. STATE OF HARYANA, 2021

**Hon'ble Judges/Coram:** U.U. Lalit and Indira Banerjee, JJ.

**Act/ Sections:** Code of Criminal Procedure, 1973 (CrPC) - Section 161; Indian Penal Code, 1860 (IPC) - Section 34, Indian Penal Code, 1860 (IPC) - Section 120B, Indian Penal Code, 1860 (IPC) - Section 216, Indian Penal Code, 1860 (IPC) - Section 302, Indian Penal Code, 1860 (IPC) - Section 364A, Indian Penal Code, 1860 (IPC) - Section 376

**No. of pages of the Original Judgement: 07**

**Citation:** AIR2021SC1904, (2021)5SCC730, MANU/SC/0242/2021

**Case Note:** Criminal - Acquittal - Lack of evidence - Sections 34, 120-B, 216, 364-A and 376 of Indian Penal Code, 1860 - FIR was registered against accused persons in respect of the offences punishable Under Sections 302,364-A,376,216 read with Section 120-B of Code - On strength of material on record, Trial Court found that charge under Section 302,120-B,34 of Code was proved against certain accused persons while charges under Sections 364-A and 376 of Code were not proved against them - Convicted Accused preferred appeals before High Court challenging their conviction and sentence - High Court rejected appeals preferred by convicted accused - Hence, present appeal - Whether prosecution prove its case beyond reasonable doubt.

**Facts:** An FIR was registered in respect of the offences punishable under Sections 302,364-A,376,216 read with Section 120-B of the Indian Penal Code,

1860. The Investigating Officer deposed regarding the facts concerning recoveries pursuant to the disclosure statements made by the Accused. On the strength of the material on record, the Trial Court by its judgment and order found that the charge under Section 302/120-B/34 Indian Penal Code was proved against the certain accused persons while the charges under Sections 364-A and 376 Indian Penal Code were not proved against them, rest of the Accused were not found guilty of any of the charges levelled against them and hence were acquitted. The convicted Accused preferred appeals before the High Court challenging their conviction and sentence which was rejected.

**Hon'ble Apex Court Held, while allowing the appeal:** (i) The evidence on record discloses that out of three witnesses, who were stated to be the eye-witnesses, two witnesses, turned hostile and did not support the case of the prosecution. Both these witnesses were close relations of the victim and there is nothing on record to indicate that they were either put under any pressure or that there was any element of suspicion. Both these witnesses were categorical that the persons who kidnapped the victim were not before the Court in the capacity as the Accused.

(ii) This court were thus left with the testimony of the informant and the father of the victim. The reporting made by this witness, based on which the crime was registered neither shows that he was an eye-witness to the occurrence nor does it disclose that the identity of the Accused who had kidnapped the victim was in any way known at the stage when the occurrence took place. The statement given by the witness in his cross-examination further discloses that he was sitting inside the house when the incident had occurred and that the shouts of the children and other passers-by had attracted his attention whereafter the witness came out of the house. In the circumstances, it was extremely difficult to accept informant to be an eye-witness to the occurrence. The observations made by the High Court while placing reliance on his version, were totally incorrect. Thus, all three witnesses who were claimed to be the eye-witnesses to the occurrence and on whose testimonies, reliance was placed by the prosecution, were of no help.

(iii) There were of course circumstances like recovery of clothing apparel as well as tiffin box etc. belonging to the victim. However, such recoveries by themselves, in the absence of any other material evidence on record pointing towards the guilt of the Accused, could not be termed sufficient to hold that the case was proved beyond reasonable doubt. Not only those circumstances were not conclusive in nature but they also did not form a cogent and consistent chain to exclude every other hypothesis except the guilt of the Appellants.

(iv) The case of the prosecution had not been proved beyond reasonable doubt, and the Appellants were entitled to the benefit of doubt. MANU/SC/8150/2006

❦❦❦

# TEN

# OM PRAKASH VS. STATE OF U.P., 2006

**Hon'ble Judges/Coram:** Dr. Arijit Pasayat and S.H. Kapadia, JJ.

**Citation:** AIR2006SC2214, AIR2006SC2214, (2006)9SCC787, [2006] Supp(2)SCR318, MANU/SC/8150/2006

**Act/ Sections:** Code of Criminal Procedure, 1973 (CrPC) - Section 313; Indian Evidence Act, 1872 - Section 114, Indian Evidence Act, 1872 - Section 118; Indian Penal Code 1860, (IPC) - Section 228A; Indian Penal Code 1860, (IPC) - Section 376; Indian Penal Code 1860, (IPC) - Section 376(1); Indian Penal Code 1860, (IPC) - Section 376(2)(e); Indian Penal Code 1860, (IPC) - Section 376A; Indian Penal Code 1860, (IPC) - Section 376B; Indian Penal Code 1860, (IPC) - Section 376C; Indian Penal Code 1860, (IPC) - Section 376D

**No. of pages of the Original Judgement: 06**

**Case Note:** Indian Penal Code, 1860 - Sections 376 (1) and 376 (2) (e) Rape Conviction and sentence Whether no corroboration to testimony of prosecutrix required when it is trustworthy? Held, "yes" No evidence to show that accused knew that prosecutrix was pregnant Hence, Section 376 (2) (e) not attracted--Case falls under Section 376 (1) Accordingly, sentence reduced to 7 years from 10 years.

**Facts:** It is settled law that the victim of sexual assault is not treated as accomplice and as such, her evidence does not require corroboration from any other evidence including the evidence of a doctor. In a given case even if the doctor who examined the victim does not find sign of rape, it is no ground to disbelieve the sole testimony of the prosecutrix. In normal course, a victim of sexual assault does not like to disclose such offence even before her family members, much less before public or before the police.

The Indian woman has tendency to conceal such offence because it involves her prestige as well as prestige of her family. Only in few cases, the victim girl or the family members have courage to go before the police and lodge a case. In the instant case, the suggestion given on behalf of the defence that the victim has falsely implicated the accused does not appeal to reasoning. There was no apparent reason for a married woman to falsely implicate the accused after scatting her own prestige and honour.

**Hon'ble Apex court Held, while Dispossing the appeal:** The Court must be conscious of the fact that it is dealing with the evidence of a person who is interested in the outcome of the charge levelled by her. If the Court keeps this in mind and feels satisfied that it can act on the evidence of the prosecutrix, there is no rule of law or practice incorporated in the Indian Evidence Act, 1872 similar to Illustration (b) to Section 114 which requires it to look for corroboration. If for some reason the Court is hesitant to place implicit reliance on the testimony of the prosecutrix it may look for evidence which may lend assurance to her testimony short of corroboration required in the case of an accomplice. The nature of evidence required to lend assurance to the testimony of the prosecutrix must necessarily depend on the facts and circumstances of each case. But if a prosecutrix is an adult and of full understanding the Court is entitled to base a conviction on her evidence unless the same is shown to be infirm and not trustworthy. If the totality of the circumstances appearing on the record of the case discloses that the prosecutrix does not have a strong motive to falsely involve the person charged, the Court should ordinarily have no hesitation in accepting her evidence.

While considering the case covered by Section 376 (2) (e), what is needed to be seen is whether evidence establishes knowledge of the accused. Mere possibility of knowledge is not sufficient. When a case relates to one where because of the serious nature of the offence, as statutorily prescribed, more stringent sentence is provided, it must be established and not a possibility is to be inferred. The language of Section 376 (2) (e) is clear. It requires prosecution to establish that the accused knew her to be pregnant. This is clear from the use of the expression "knowing her to be pregnant". This is conceptually different from that there is a possibility of his knowledge or that probably he knew it. Positive evidence has to be adduced by the prosecution about the knowledge. In the absence of any material brought on record to show that the accused knew the victim to be pregnant Section 376 (2) (e), I.P.C. cannot be pressed into service. To that extent, the judgment of the courts below is unsustainable. However, minimum sentence prescribed under Section 376 (1), I.P.C. is clearly applicable.

ᏢᏢᏢ

# ELEVEN

# PRADEEP RAM VS. THE STATE OF JHARKHAND AND ORS., 2019

**Hon'ble Judges/Coram:** Ashok Bhushan and K.M. Joseph, JJ.

**Act/ Sections**: Code of Criminal Procedure, 1973 (CrPC) - Section 167; Code of Criminal Procedure, 1973 (CrPC) - Section 309(2)(I PC) - Section 376A, Indian Penal Code 1860, (IPC) - Section 376AB, Indian Penal Code 1860, (IPC) - Section 376B, Indian Penal Code 1860, (IPC) - Section 376C, Indian Penal Code 1860, (IPC) - Section 376D, Indian Penal Code 1860, (IPC) - Section 376DA, Indian Penal Code 1860, (IPC) - Section 376DB

**No. of pages of the original Judgement: 023**

**Citation:** AIR2019SC3193, (2019)17SCC326, MANU/SC/0881/2019

**Case Note**: Criminal - Quashing of proceedings - Entitlement to - Sections 482, 167, 437, 439 and 309(2) of Code of Criminal Procedure, 1973 (CrPC) and Sections 16, 17, 20 and 23 of Unlawful Activities (Prevention) Act, 1967 and Section 6(5) and 8 of National Investigation Agency Act, 2008 - Present appeals had been filed against judgment of High Court dismissing Writ Petition under Section 482 of CrPC filed by Appellant - Whether in a case where an Accused had been bailed out in a criminal case, in which case, subsequently new offences were added, was it necessary that, bail earlier granted should be cancelled for taking Accused in custody - Whether re-registration of F.I.R. was a second F.I. R. and was not permissible there being already a FIR registered arising out of same incident - Whether N.I. A. could conduct any further investigation in matter, when investigation in the P.S. Case having already been completed and charge sheet had been submitted on with regard to which cognizance had already been taken by Chief Judicial Magistrate - Whether order passed by Judicial Commissioner-cum-Special Judge, NIA, Ranchi remanding Appellant to judicial custody was in accordance with law - Whether power under Section 167 of CrPC could be exercised in present case, where cognizance had already been taken by Chief Judicial Magistrate on 11th March, 2016 or Accused could have been remanded only under Section 309(2) of CrPC.

**Facts**: First Information Report was lodged for offences under Sections 414, 384, 386, 387, 120-B Indian Penal Code, 1860 (IPC) read with Sections 25(1-B)(a), 26, 35 of the Arms Act and Section 17(1) and (2) of the Criminal Law Amendment Act. Apart from Petitioner, there were 11 other named Accused. The allegations made against the Accused were that, Applicant by showing fear of extremist of TPC Group recovered levy from the contractors, transporters, and coal businessman. It was also alleged that on information received from a co-Accused, a search was also conducted in the house of the Appellant, during which search, an amount of Rs. 57,57,510 was recovered from the bag kept in the room of the Appellant along with four mobiles. No satisfactory explanation was given by the Appellant. Thereafter, on the prayer made by the Investigating Officer, offences under Sections 16, 17, 20 and 23 of the Act, 1967 were added against the Accused. Central Government issued an order in exercise of power conferred under Sub-section 5 of Section 6 read with Section 8 of the National Investigation Agency Act, 2008 suo-moto directing the National Investigation Agency to take up investigation of case F.I.R., in which Sections 16, 17, 20 and 23 of Act, 1967 were added, which were scheduled offences. In pursuance of the order of the Central Government, National Investigation Agency re-registered the First Information Report as FIR dated 16th February, 2018. A Writ Petition was filed by the Appellant praying for quashing the entire criminal proceedings in connection with Special NIA Case including the First Information Report. A further prayer was also made for quashing the order remanding the Appellant to the judicial custody by order of the Judicial Commissioner-cum-Special Judge, NIA. The High Court by the impugned judgment dismissed both, the Writ Petition, aggrieved against which judgment, present appeals have been filed by the Appellant.

**Hon'ble Apex Court Held, while dismissing the appeals**: 1. Appellant was already into jail custody with regard to another case and the investigating agency applied before Special Judge, NIA Court to grant production warrant to produce the Accused before the Court. The Special Judge having accepted the prayer of grant of production warrant, the Accused was produced before the Court on 26th June, 2018 and remanded to custody. Thus, in the present case, production of the Accused was with the permission of the Court. Thus, the present is not a case where investigating agency itself has taken into custody the Appellant after addition of new offences rather Accused was produced in the Court in pursuance of production warrant obtained from the Court by the investigating agency. There is no error in the procedure which was adopted by the Special Judge, NIA Court with regard to production of Appellant before the Court. In the facts of the present case, it was not necessary for the Special Judge to pass an order cancelling the bail granted to the Appellant before permitting the Accused Appellant to be produced before it or remanding him to the judicial custody.

2. The Accused can surrender and apply for bail for newly added cognizable and non-bailable offences. In event of refusal of bail, the Accused can certainly be arrested. The investigating agency can seek order from the court under Section 437(5) or 439(2) of CrPC for arrest of the Accused and his custody. The Court, in exercise of power under Section 437(5) or 439(2) of CrPC, can direct for taking into custody the Accused who has already been granted bail after cancellation of his bail. The Court in exercise of power under Section 437(5) as well as Section 439(2) can direct the person who has already been granted bail to be arrested and commit him to custody on addition of graver and non-cognizable offences which may not be necessary always with order of cancelling of earlier bail. In a case where an Accused has already been granted bail, the investigating authority on addition of an offence or offences may not proceed to arrest the Accused, but for arresting the Accused on such addition of offence or offences it needs to obtain an order to arrest the Accused from the Court which had granted the bail.

3. There cannot be any dispute to the proposition that, second FIR with regard to same offences is barred. But whether in the present case, FIR dated 16th February, 2018 registered by NIA, can be said to be second FIR.

4. NIA Act, 2008 was enacted to constitute an investigation agency at the national level to investigate and prosecute offences affecting the sovereignty, security and integrity of India, security of State, friendly relations with foreign States and offences under Acts enacted to implement international treaties, agreements, conventions and resolutions of the United Nations, its agencies and other international organizations and for

matters connected therewith or incidental thereto.

5. Any offence under Act, 1967 is a scheduled offence. When the offences under the Act, 1967 were added in case Crime No. 02/2016 and that the Central Government order issued in exercise of its power under Sub-section 5 of Section 6 by entrusting the investigation to NIA, NIA is competent to investigate the offence and submit a supplementary report.

6. A charge sheet in the case Crime was submitted by the investigating agency and cognizance was taken. The offences under Act, 1967 were added. Charges were framed on 19th September, 2016, offences under Act, 1967 were added for the first time on 09.04.2017, thus, there was no occasion for investigation of offences under Act, 1967 prior to April, 2017. The charge sheet dated 10th March, 2016 and charges framed on 19th September,2016 were not with respect to offences under Act, 1967, thus, when the Central Government directed the NIA to investigate the offence under scheduled offences, NIA was fully competent to investigate the offences and submit a supplementary report. Present is not a case where any charges for offences punishable under the Unlawful Activities (Prevention) Act, 1967 were available prior to April, 2017, thus, NIA was fully competent to investigate further in the case as per the directions issued by the Central Government vide order.

7. Sub-section (6) of Section 6, prohibits State Government or any police officer of the State Government to proceed with the investigation. In the present case, when order was issued by Central Government on 13th February, 2018, it was not competent for police officer of the State Government to proceed with the investigation. FIR, which was re-registered by NIA on 16th February, 2018 cannot be held to be second FIR of the offences rather it was re-registration of the FIR to give effect to the provisions of the NIA Act and re-registration of the FIR is only procedural Act to initiate the investigation and the trial under the NIA Act. The re-registration of the FIR, thus, is neither barred nor can be held that it is second FIR.

8. There is no lack of jurisdiction in NIA to carry on further investigation and submit a supplementary report. In the counter affidavit, it has been stated by the Union of India that, NIA has concluded investigation and already a charge sheet has been submitted vide first supplementary charge sheet.

9. The Accused can be remanded under Section 167(2) of CrPC during investigation till cognizance has not been taken by the Court. Even after taking cognizance when an Accused is subsequently arrested during further

investigation, the Accused can be remanded under Section 167(2) of CrPC. When cognizance has been taken and the Accused was in custody at the time of taking cognizance or when inquiry or trial was being held in respect of him, he can be remanded to judicial custody only Under Section 309(2) Code of Criminal Procedure.

10. In the present case, accused could have been remanded only under Section 309(2) of CrPC.

11. The special Judge in his order has neither referred to Section 309 nor Section 167 under which Accused was remanded. When the Court has power to pass a particular order, non-mention of provision of law or wrong mention of provision of law is inconsequential. The special Judge could have only exercised power under Section 309(2); hence, the remand order has to be treated as remand order under Section 309(2) of CrPC. The special Judge being empowered to remand the Accused under Section 309(2) in the facts of the present case, there is no illegality in the remand order, when the Accused was remanded to the judicial custody.

12. The High Court, thus, committed error in holding that, the order of remand was in exercise of power under Section 167 of CrPC. The remand order was in exercise of power under Section 309(2). The remand order is upheld.

13. Appeals dismissed.

**Ratio Decidendi**: Re-registration of the FIR is neither barred nor can be held that, it is second FIR.

ᑭᑭᑭ

# TWELVE

# KADAMANIAN VS. STATE, 2016

**Hon'ble Judges/Coram**: J.S. Khehar and Arun Mishra, JJ.

**Act/ Sections:** Indian Penal Code, 1860 (IPC) - Section 201, Indian Penal Code, 1860 (IPC) - Section 302, Indian Penal Code, 1860 (IPC) - Section 376, Indian Penal Code, 1860 (IPC) - Section 404; Code of Criminal Procedure, 1973 (CrPC) - Section 161, Code of Criminal Procedure, 1973 (CrPC) - Section 164, Code of Criminal Procedure, 1973 (CrPC) - Section 313

**No. of pages of the Original Judgement**: 013

**Citation:** AIR2016SC4266, AIR2016SC4266, MANU/SC/0970/2016

**Case Note:** Criminal - Legality of Conviction of Appellant - Prosecution lodged against Appellant herein - As well as against co-accused-I.T.Manian - Offences Under Sections 201, 302, 376 and 404, Indian Penal Code - Prosecution version - M. Jayalakshmi went missing - Missing person's report lodged - In First Information Report so registered - Complainant attached photograph of Jayalakshmi - For her identification - Expressly mentioned - Wearing a nose-stud - Later, a dead body of female found - Another First Information Report lodged - Parents of deceased-Jayalakshmi identified the clothing and other artefacts - Recovered with the dead body - Belonging to their daughter - Identification affirmed by the mother of the deceased - First needle of suspicion - Reference to Appellant - Emerged from statement of Investigating officer-PW20 - Affirming with PW6 - Appellant been seen close to place of occurrence - Consequently, Appellant made an extra-judicial confession - R.V. Alagurajan-PW12 - After PW-12 effectuated surrender of accused-Appellant - Inspector of Police - PW12 also submitted a letter at police station - Accused-Appellant made confessional statement - After being produced before Inspector of Police - Prosecution's version - Based on statement made by Appellant - Nose-stud recovered - Instance of Appellant - Fact that same belonged to deceased - Confirmed by various witnesses - Including PW-2, mother of the deceased - After recording statements of prosecution witnesses - Also of accused - Section 313 of Code of Criminal Procedure - Accused afforded an opportunity - Lead evidence in defence - Accused availed off the opportunity - Trial Court rendered its judgment - Convicted both the accused - Offences levelled against them - Dissatisfied, both Appellants preferred Criminal Appeal - Division Bench of High Court - Accepted appeal preferred by accused No. 2-I.T. Manian - Ordered his acquittal - Appeal preferred by Appellant - Dismissed - Present appeal against Division Bench's judgment and order - Whether the non-recording of the extra-judicial confession over a span of time, in the facts of the present case, was consequential - Whether the High Court was correct in acquitting the co-accused while dismissing the Appellant's appeal - Whether the submission of the learned Counsel for Appellant that absence of any human tissue on the nose-pin lead to the inference that nose-pin in question was not the one belonging to the deceased, tenable in law - Whether the High Court was correct and justified in upholding the conviction of the Appellant

**Facts**: The prosecution in the instant case was lodged against the Appellant herein-Kadamanian @ Manikandan, as well as, against co-accused-I.T. Manian @ Manikanda, for the offences Under Sections 201, 302, 376 and 404 of the Indian Penal Code. The aforesaid offences were allegedly committed by the accused with reference to M. Jayalakshmi.

As per the prosecution version, M. Jayalakshmi went missing, having left her residence to answer the call of nature. Since she did not return, a missing person's report was lodged the next day by her father P. Matheswaran at Police Station. In the first information report so registered, the complainant had attached the photograph of M. Jayalakshmi, and had also indicated for her identification, that she was wearing a green colour jacket and saree. It was also expressly mentioned, that she was wearing a nose-stud.

Later, a dead body of a female, was found by a sweeper, Natarajan - PW4. Based on the recovery of the dead body, another first information report came to be lodged. The parents of the deceased-Jayalakshmi, identified the clothing and other artifacts, recovered with the dead body, as belonging to their daughter. The aforesaid identification was affirmed by none other than the mother of the deceased, Vedammal - PW2. The mother identified her daughter from the photograph of the dead body.

The first needle of suspicion with reference to the Appellant herein emerged from the statement of the investigating officer, Arumugam - PW20 affirming with Shanmugam - PW6, that the Appellant had been seen close to the place of occurrence. Consequent upon the needle of suspicion having been pointed at the Appellant, the Appellant allegedly made an extra-judicial confession to R.V. Alagurajan - PW12.

After PW-12 had allegedly effectuated the surrender of the accused-Appellant before the Inspector of Police, he had also submitted a letter at the police station. Consequent upon the Appellant having been produced before the Inspector of Police, the accused-Appellant made a confessional statement on the same day.

It is the version of the prosecution, that based on the statement made by the Appellant, a nose-stud was recovered at the instance of the Appellant on 22.01.2008. The fact that the same belong to the deceased-Jayalakshmi was confirmed by various witnesses including PW2 - Vedammal, the mother of the deceased. After recording the statements of the prosecution witnesses, and also, the statement of the accused Under Section 313 of the Code of Criminal Procedure, the accused were afforded an opportunity to lead their evidence in defence. The accused availed off the above opportunity, and thereafter, the trial Court rendered its judgment convicting both the accused of the offences levelled against them.

Dissatisfied with the order passed by the Trial Court, both the Appellants preferred Criminal Appeal before the High Court. A Division Bench of High Court accepted the appeal preferred by accused No. 2 - I.T. Manian and ordered his acquittal. The appeal preferred by the Appellant herein was dismissed. Although, the sentences awarded by the trial Court, under various provisions of the Indian Penal Code, were by and large maintained, the sentence awarded to the Appellant (by the trial Court) Under Section 376 of the Indian Penal Code was reduced from 10 years to 7 years. Present appeal has been filed against the judgment and order of the Division Bench.

**Hon'ble Apex Court Held, while dismissing the appeal**: 1. During the course of hearing, learned Counsel for the Appellant raised various contentions. First and foremost, it was sought to be canvassed, that there was no direct or ocular evidence recorded at the behest of the prosecution, so as to render clear and unambiguous culpability of the Appellant. It was pointed out, that the conviction of the Appellant by the trial Court, as also, by the High Court, was based only on circumstantial evidence. The most relevant circumstantial evidence taken into consideration by the High Court, according to learned Counsel, was the extra-judicial confession made by the Appellant, to R.V. Alagurajan - PW12 on 22.1.2008. The details of the aforesaid confessional statement have already been recorded by the Court hereinabove.

2. It was the submission of the learned Counsel for the Appellant, that R.V. Alagurajan - PW12 was a stark stranger to the Appellant, and therefore, there was no occasion for the Appellant, to have made a confessional statement to him. It was submitted, that in any case, keeping in mind the fact, that the deceased - Jayalakshmi had gone missing on 6.9.2007, there was no justification for the accused - Appellant to have made a confessional statement month thereafter, on 22.1.2008.

3. The Court would have ordinarily dealt with the instant submission by itself. However, during the course of hearing, the same was sought to be linked with another submission advanced at the hands of the learned Counsel for the Appellant, namely, the recovery of the nose-stud at the behest of the confessional statement made by the accused-Appellant to the Inspector Arumugam - PW20 on 22.1.2008. It was the contention of the learned Counsel for the Appellant, that the nose-stud recovered at the behest of the Appellant, weighted only 0.215 mg. It was pointed out, that there are thousands of such nose-pins, and it was wholly improper for the prosecution to rely on the trumped-up recovery of a nose-pin. It was submitted, that it was the case of the prosecution itself, that the nose-pin in question was of the value of just about Rs. 450/-

4. The more vigorous submission with reference to the nose-pin was, that the case of the prosecution, that the Appellant herein, as also, the co-accused had badly mutilated the face of the deceased - Jayalakshmi, by crushing her face with stones, and as such, there was no question of the recovery of the nose-pin form a mutilated face. It was submitted, that if the accused had taken the nose-pin after mutilating the face of the accused, the nose-pin ought to have had fragments of skin, bone and blood. However, the nose-pin recovered was clean and without any human tissue. It was also submitted, that the nose-pin, which was allegedly recovered at the instance of the Appellant, was perfectly intact. In this behalf, it was pointed out, that if the face of the deceased - Jayalakshmi was crushed with stones, the nose-pin could not be expected to have retained its original shape.

5. The Court gave its thoughtful consideration to the two submissions advanced at the hands of the learned Counsel for the Appellant. Insofar as

the extra-judicial confession is concerned, it is necessary to emphasize, that the non-recording of the extra-judicial confession over a span of time, in the facts of the present case, was inconsequential. The Court said so, because the Appellant was not a suspect till 21.1.2008. The Appellant feared his arrest with reference to the allegations pertaining to the deceased - Jayalakshmi, only when the investigating officer, Arumugam - PW20 affirmed with Shanmugam - PW6 on 21.01.2008, that the Appellant had been seen, close to the place of occurrence. It is immediately thereafter, and on the immediately following day, that the Appellant made an extra-judicial confession to R.V. Alagurajan - PW12.

6. It is also not a matter of dispute, that R.V. Alagurajan - PW12 was the then Village Administrative Officer. It is obvious, that the aforesaid extra-judicial confession was made as is apparent from the statement of the Appellant (extracted hereinabove) to save himself from any adverse, physical handling by the investigating authorities. Undoubtedly, R.V. Alagurajan - PW12, the Village Administrative Officer, effectuated the aforesaid object, by accompanying the Appellant to the police station, and ensuring his arrest at the hands of Arumugam - PW20.

7. Insofar as the submissions advanced at the hands of the learned Counsel for the Appellant with reference to the nose-pin are concerned, the Court was of the view, that none of the contentions advanced on behalf of the Appellant, can be accepted as a valid justification, for exculpating the Appellant from the charges levelled against him. In this behalf, it would be relevant to mention, that a missing person's report was registered by the father of the deceased - P. Matheswaran, on 7.9.2007. In the missing person's report, it was clearly mentioned, that the deceased was wearing a nose-pin when she had gone missing. The reason for indicating, that the deceased was wearing a nose-pin, was with the clear purpose of aiding the identification of his missing daughter - Jayalakshmi. This was obviously for the reason, that the deceased - Jayalakshmi, was mentally unstable, and would not have been in a position to express her identification, or the identification of her parents, or the place of her residence, by herself.

8. In the recovery mahazar dated 22.1.2008, the recovered nose-pin was depicted as being imbedded with four white stones. It is therefore apparent, that the nose-pin worn by the deceased - Jayalakshmi when she had gone

missing, was not any ordinary unidentifiable artifact, but was clearly different from the usual nose-studs. Not only that, the photograph of the deceased submitted along with the missing person's report dated 7.9.2007 shows a clear picture of the nose-pin, and therefore, to say that the involvement of the accused on the basis of the nose-pin, was improper, is not acceptable. Insofar as the absence of blood, skin tissue and bone tissue on the nose-pin is concerned, it is clear to the Court, that the submissions were made by the learned Counsel, without having viewed the photograph of the deceased, as is available on the record of the trial Court. As already noticed hereinabove, the nose-pin was worn by the deceased - Jayalakshmi, in the photograph attached to the missing person's report dated 7.9.2007. The same was missing from the photograph of the deceased, after her body was recovered. The nose itself was not mutilated, and was intact. No injury whatsoever was found on the nose, in the photograph of the deceased. It was therefore wholly unjustified, for the learned Counsel for the Appellant to have raised the submission, that the absence of any human tissue on the nose-pin, would lead to the inference, that the nose-pin in question, was not the one belonging to the deceased. For the reasons recorded hereinabove, the Court found no merit in the instant contentions, advanced on behalf of the Appellant.

9. Insofar as the veracity of the extra judicial confession made by the Appellant is concerned, it would be relevant to mention that, learned Counsel, during the course of hearing, placed reliance on a judgment rendered by this Court in Kala @ Chandrakala v. State through Inspector of Police. Based on the aforesaid judgment rendered by this Court, it was submitted, that the extra-judicial confession being a weak piece of evidence, should not have been relied upon, for determining the culpability of the Appellant.

10. Having given its thoughtful consideration on the above contention, the Court was of the view, that the judgment relied upon by learned Counsel, is wholly inapplicable in the facts and circumstances of this case, for two distinguishing features in the present case, namely, that the extra judicial confession in the instant case was made to the Village Administrative Officer R.V. Alagurajan - PW12, who was totally unbiased and unconnected with the controversy in hand. He could also not to be stated to be inimical to the Appellant. He is not shown to have any relationship with either the complainant or the accused. Moreover, insofar as the extra judicial confession made in the judgment relied upon by the Appellant is concerned,

the same had been made by the accused, to the sister of the deceased, which by itself made the extra judicial confession extremely doubtful. The Court was, therefore, not impressed with the submission advanced by the learned Counsel for the Appellant, based on the cited judgment.

11. The next contention advanced at the hands of the learned Counsel for the Appellant was, on the third circumstantial evidence taking into consideration, namely, the last seen evidence. For establishing the above circumstance, the prosecution had relied upon two witnesses, Shanmugam - PW6, and Mubarak - PW7. In the statements recorded by the aforesaid two witnesses Under Section 161 of the Code of Criminal Procedure, they had stated, that they had seen the Appellant and the co-accused in the company of the deceased - Jayalakshmi. While recording their statements before the trial Court, Shanmugam - PW6 and Mubarak - PW7 resiled from the version indicated by them, to the investigating officer. It is therefore apparent, that no last seen evidence, could be substantiated by the prosecution, during the course of the trial of the Appellant.

12. The Court was of the view, that the deposition at the hands of Shanmugam - PW6 and Mubarak - PW7, can be described as a matter of improper handling of the case, inasmuch as, both Shanmugam - PW6 and Mubarak - PW7 had also recorded their statements Under Section 164 of the Code of Criminal Procedure, affirming, that they had seen the Appellant and the co-accused in the company of the deceased - Jayalakshmi. However, since the statement of the two prosecution witnesses recorded Under Sections 161 and 164 of the Code of Criminal Procedure, was not put to them, after they were declared hostile, and were subjected to cross-examination at the behest of the prosecution, the Court had no alternative, but to overlook the last seen evidence sought to be projected by the prosecution.

13. In the above view of the matter, it was the contention of the learned Counsel for the Appellant, that there was no material evidence available on the record of the case, to return a clear finding of guilt, against the Appellant. It was submitted, that the circumstantial evidence projected through the prosecution witnesses, did not complete the chain of circumstances, as would establish the guilt of the Appellant. The Court has given its thoughtful consideration to the submissions advanced at the hands of the learned Counsel for the Appellant. As noticed hereinabove, there was a clear and categoric extra-judicial confession made by the Appellant to R.V. Alagurajan - PW12 on 22.1.2008. During the course of recording his testimony, R.V.

Alagurajan - PW12 was subjected to vigorous cross-examination. His testimony however remained unshaken. Resultantly, the trial Court, as also, the High Court, concluded that the extra-judicial confession was genuine. The Court endorsed the above determination at the hands of the trial Court and the High Court.

14. Consequent upon the accused-appellant's extra-judicial confession, the Appellant was taken to the police station by R.V. Alagurajan - PW12, and produced before Inspector Arumugam - PW20. It is therefore apparent, that the arrest of the Appellant at the behest of R.V. Alagurajan - PW12, has also been clearly established. The next chain in the circumstantial evidence projected at the hands of the prosecution, was the recovery of the nose-pin on 22.1.2008, based on the statement of the Appellant, to Inspector Arumugam - PW20. The afore-stated nose-pin has been identified by the members of the family of the deceased, as the one that was actually worn by the deceased, when she went missing. Since the nose-pin was recovered at the instance of the Appellant, from a remote place under an electric transformer, no one but the Appellant could have been aware of its location. Its recovery was therefore sufficient, along with the other evidence referred to above, to clearly implicate the Appellant.

15. The Court felt it necessary to mention, that there is yet another aspect of the matter, which furthers the cause of the prosecution, namely, the statement of M. Abdul Khader - PW8. In this behalf, it would be relevant to mention, that the Appellant used to hire a share-autorickshaw, for earning his livelihood. The aforesaid autorickshaw was hired from the garage of Annamalai - PW9. M. Abdul Khader - PW8 was engaged as an accountant at the garage of Annamalai - PW9. It was pointed out in the deposition of M. Abdul Khader - PW8, that on a daily basis the share-autorickshaw hired by the accused-Appellant and the co-accused used to be returned to the garage of Annamalai - PW9 between 8.30 p.m. to 9.30 p.m. However, on the date of occurrence, i.e., the relevant date when the alleged crime was committed, the share-autorickshaw was returned on the following day, at 1.30 a.m. The case of the prosecution is, that the autorickshaw was used by the Appellant and the co-accused in commission of the crime. It was imperative for the Appellant to have expressly indicated the reasons and justification for not returning the autorickshaw to the garage of Annamalai - PW9 between 8.30 p.m. to 9.30 p.m., on the relevant date. Not having done so, by itself, is a cause of suspicion, especially when there is other material evidence, projected by the prosecution, to demonstrate the involvement of the Appellant, in the

commission of the crime. The Court was of the view, that the aforesaid evidence recorded by the prosecution was sufficient, even in the absence of last seen evidence, to return a finding of guilt against the Appellant.

16. It is imperative for the Court to record, that in addition to the afore-stated submissions advanced at the hands of the learned Counsel for the Appellant, learned Counsel had also contended, that the co-accused was acquitted by the High Court, and that, his acquittal was based on the same evidence, produced through the same witnesses. It was contended, that it was improper and unjustified, for the High Court, to have convicted the Appellant, and acquitted the co-accused, on the same evidence. The Court found no justification in the instant contention advanced at the hands of the learned Counsel. The Court has already recorded hereinabove, that the extra judicial confession made to R.V. Alagurajan - PW12, was by the Appellant herein, and not by the co-accused. The Court has also recorded hereinabove that the recovery of the nose-pin found missing from the nose of the deceased, was at the instance of the Appellant, and not at the hands of the co-accused. Therefore, the case of the co-accused, was on a clearly different footing, and there was sufficient justification for the High Court, to have taken a different view, SW in the case of the co-accused.

For the reasons recorded hereinabove, the Court found no justification whatsoever to interfere with the conviction and sentence awarded to the Appellant, by the High Court. The instant appeal was accordingly dismissed.

ppp

# THIRTEEN

# Parkash Chand Vs. State of Himachal Pradesh, 2019

**Hon'ble Judges/Coram**: Ranjan Gogoi, C.J.I., Sanjay Kishan Kaul and K.M. Joseph, JJ.

**Act/ Sections**: Indian Penal Code, 1860 (IPC) - Section 376; Indian Penal Code, 1860 (IPC) - Section 506

**No. of pags of the Original Judgement: 08**

**Citation**: AIR2019SC1037, (2019)5SCC628, MANU/SC/0181/2019

**Case Note**: Criminal - Conviction - Challenge thereto - Sections 376 and 506 of Indian Penal Code, 1860 (IPC) - Present was a criminal appeal by special leave challenging order passed by High Court affirming conviction of Appellant under Sections 376 and 506 of IPC - Whether impugned order convicting Appellant was liable to be set aside.

**Facts**: In December, 1999, Appellant committed rape upon P.W. 2. It was also further case that, P.W. 2 was intimidated by Appellant and another co-accused. Appellant was charged under Sections 376 and 506 of Indian Penal Code read with Section 34 of IPC and co-accused was charged under Section 506 read with Section 34 of IPC. Trial Court found case in favour of prosecution and after convicting Appellant and co-accused sentenced Appellant to simple imprisonment for 7 years and a fine of Rs. 10,000 with default sentence for offence punishable under Section 376 of IPC. He was also sentenced for 2 years for offence punishable under Section 506 of IPC. Both sentences were to run concurrently. Co-accused stand acquitted by

High court whereas appeal filed by Appellant was unsuccessful.

**Hon'ble Apex Court Held, while allowing the appeal** 1. There was admittedly a delay of 7 months in lodging FIR in case of alleged rape. If case was reported immediately apart from inherent strength of case flowing from genuineness attributable to such promptitude, perceptible advantage would be medical examination to which prosecutrix could be subjected and result of such examination in a case where there was a resistance. It was case of prosecution that, she raised hue and cry and therefore apparently, she would have resisted. Possibly, a medical examination might have revealed signs of any resistance or injuries. In this case, High Court had proceeded on basis of testimony of prosecutrix and sought to fortify it by extra judicial confession made before PW4 and PW5.

2. If evidence adduced by prosecution fell short of test of reliability and acceptability and as such it was highly unreliable to act upon it even in an appeal by special leave, such a critical examination might not be unwarranted. Also, when vital evidence was not appreciated, present Court could interfere. Furthermore, trial court, in fact, proceeded on basis that, prosecutrix was not a minor. High Court found on evidence that, prosecutrix was not a minor.

3. Incident was alleged to have taken place near a path which had been admitted by the prosecutrix and her aunt PW3 as common path. If indeed prosecutrix had raised hue and cry, it was very unlikely that, laborer's who were supposed to haunt the common path could not hear it. In circumstances of this case, Appellant could not be convicted for offence under Section 376. It would indeed be unsafe to convict him based on testimony of prosecutrix. He would certainly be entitled to benefit of doubt which was created by very circumstances referred.

4. Trial Court, in fact, has proceeded to rely upon testimony of prosecutrix about Appellant threatening her that in case she disclosed incident to anyone she would be killed by Accused. This apparently was related to incident in December, 1999. In fact, Appellant was specifically charged with criminal intimidation allegedly done on 10th july, 2000. Appellant was so charged in alleged furtherance of common intention along with co-accused. Trial Court had also proceeded to convict co-accused relying on evidence of prosecutrix. High Court had acquitted co-accused of charge of criminal intimidation. There was no specific charge even framed against Appellant under Section 506 in regard to alleged incident which took place in December, 1999 and charge in fact related only to acts alleged

to have been committed on 10th July, 2000. Apart from fact that, there was no specific charge against Appellant in regard to what happened in December, 1999, Appellant could not be convicted under Section 506 having regard to circumstances.

5. Order of conviction and sentence of Appellant by Courts below was set aside. Appeal allowed.

ÞÞÞ

# FOURTEEN

# STATE OF RAJASTHAN VS. NOORE KHAN, 2000

**Hon'ble Judges/Coram**: Dr. A.S. Anand, C.J.I., R.C. Lahoti and S.N. Variava, JJ.

**Act/ Sections**: Evidence Act - Section 8, Evidence Act - Section 157; Indian Penal Code, 1860 (IPC) - Section 375, Indian Penal Code, 1860 (IPC) - Section 376

**No. of pages of the original Judgement**: 08

**Citation**: MANU/SC/3475/2000

**Case Note**: Criminal - Appeal against Acquittal - Accused-Respondent was found guilty by Trial Court of committing offence punishable Under Section 376 of the Indian Penal Code, 1860 - High Court vide impugned judgment reversed the judgment holding that the prosecutrix was not proved beyond reasonable doubt to be below 16 years of age - Whether the High Court erred in directing acquittal of the Respondent?

**Facts**: According to the prosecution, the prosecutrix, aged 15 years was living in village with her father, mother, and a younger sister. The family resided in a lonely hutment situated in a field. On the date of incident, the prosecutrix was alone in her hut busy washing clothes on a water pump. NK, the accused-Respondent was known to the prosecutrix since before. He came to her and initially asked for water which she provided in a lota. The accused then asked for a knife for peeling the skin of a cucumber. The prosecutrix brought the knife and handed it over to him. When the prosecutrix was about to turn and go back, the accused caught hold to her. He twisted her hand on her back and forcibly took her to a nearby place. The accused forced the prosecutrix to lie down on the ground, put his foot on her chest, closed her mouth with his palm, removed her lehenga upwards and then forcibly committed sexual intercourse with her. The prosecutrix offered resistance and tried to save herself but the Respondent gagged her mouth by a towel pressed against her mouth. Having thus raped the prosecutrix, the accused-Respondent went away to another village or part of the same village. The prosecutrix reached back her home and narrated the entire incident to her father, PW 10, who had returned by that time. The victim accompanied by her father wanted to go to the police station and lodge the first information report of the incident but they were prevented from doing so by several village people belonging to the community of the accused who also proposed the matter being settled within the village by convening a panchayat. However, report of the incident was lodged and the offence was registered. The trial Court found the incident, as alleged, proved based on testimony of the prosecutrix. It was corroborated by the medical evidence and by the testimony of her father. The High Court in appeal held that the prosecutrix was not proved beyond reasonable doubt to be below 16 years of age. In the opinion of the High Court though the factum of accused-Respondent having committed sexual intercourse with the prosecutrix was proved but the absence of injuries on the person of the prosecutrix was a material fact not excluding the possibility of the prosecutrix having been a consenting party. The delay in lodging the FIR was not satisfactorily explained coupled with the non-examination of one lady to whom the incident was first narrated by the prosecutrix immediately after the occurrence rendered the prosecution case doubtful. Mainly on this reasoning High Court acquitted the accused-Respondent. Hence, the present appeal by State.

**Hon'ble Apex Court Held, While Allowing/ Disposing the Appeal:** (i) High Court was not justified in reversing the conviction of the Respondent and recording the order of acquittal.

(ii) Mere delay in lodging the FIR cannot be a ground by itself for throwing the entire prosecution case overboard. The Court has to seek an explanation for delay and test the truthfulness and plausibility of the reason assigned. If the delay is explained to the satisfaction of the Court, it cannot be counted against the prosecution.

(iii) Absence of injuries on the person of the prosecutrix has weighed with the High Court for inferring consent on the part of the prosecutrix. The prosecutrix was in her teens. The perpetrator of the crime was an able-bodied youth bustling with energy and determined to fulfill his lust armed with a knife in his hand and having succeeded in forcefully removing the victim to a secluded place where there was none around to help the prosecutrix in her defence. The injuries which the prosecutrix suffered or might have suffered in defending herself and resisting the accused were abrasions or bruises which would heal up in ordinary course of nature within 2 to 3 days of the incident. The absence of visible marks of injuries on the person of the prosecutrix on the date of her medical examination would not necessarily mean that she had not suffered any injuries or that she had offered no resistance at the time of commission of the crime. Absence of injuries on the person of the prosecutrix is not necessarily evidence of falsity of the allegation or evidence of consent on the part of the prosecutrix. It will all depend on the facts and circumstances of each case.

(iv) For the offence of rape as defined in Section 375 of the Indian Penal Code, the sexual intercourse should have been against the will of the woman or without her consent. Consent is immaterial in certain circumstances covered by clauses thirdly to sixthly, the last one being when the woman is under 16 years of age. Based on these provisions, an argument is usually advanced on behalf of the accused charged with rape that absence of proof of want of consent where the prosecutrix is not under 16 years of age takes the assault out of the purview of Section 375 of the Indian Penal Code. Certainly, consent is no defence if the victim has been proved to be under 16 years of age. If she be of 16 years of age or above, her consent cannot be presumed; an inference as to consent can be drawn if only based on evidence or probabilities of the case. The victim of rape stating on oath that she was forcibly subjected to sexual intercourse or that the act was done without her consent, has to be believed and accepted like any other testimony unless there is material available to draw an inference as to her consent or else the testimony of prosecutrix is such as would be inherently improbable. The prosecutrix had just crossed the age of 16 years. She was clearly stated that she was subjected to sexual intercourse forcibly by the accused. She was not a consenting party.

(v) High Court committed a clear error of law in interfering with the judgment of the trial Court regarding proof of guilt of the accused. The appeal was allowed.

ৡৡৡ

# FIFTEEN

# ASHOK KUMAR MEHRA AND ORS. VS. THE STATE OF PUNJAB AND ORS., 2019

**Hon'ble Judges/Coram**: Abhay Manohar Sapre and Dinesh Maheshwari, JJ.

**Act/ Sections**: Indian Penal Code, 1860 (IPC) - Section 34, Indian Penal Code, 1860 (IPC) - Section 302, Indian Penal Code, 1860 (IPC) - Section 376(2)

**No. of pages of the Original Judgement**: 04

**Citation**: AIR2019SC1903, (2019)6SCC132, MANU/SC/0535/2019

**Case Note**: Criminal - Acquittal - Juvenile - Sections 34 and 302 of Indian Penal Code, 1860 - Appellants were prosecuted for commission of offence of committing murder under Section 302 read with Section 34 of Code - Sessions Judge acquitted both Appellants - State felt aggrieved and filed criminal appeal in High Court - High Court allowed criminal appeal and convicted both Appellants and awarded them life sentence - Hence, present appeal - Whether impugned judgment of conviction warrant any interference.

**Facts**: The Appellants, i.e., father and son were prosecuted for commission of the offence of committing murder under Section 302 read with Section 34 of Indian Penal Code, 1860. The Sessions Judge by judgment/ order acquitted both the Appellants. The State felt aggrieved and filed criminal appeal in the High Court. By impugned order, the High Court allowed the criminal appeal and while reversing the judgment of acquittal passed by the Sessions Judge, convicted both the Appellants, and awarded them life sentence. So far as the Appellant No. 1- father was concerned, he had expired during the pendency of appeals.

**Hon'ble Apex Court Held, while allowing the appeal:** (i) It was an admitted fact that Appellant No. 2 was a juvenile on the date of the commission of the offence. In other words, Appellant No. 2 had not completed the age of eighteen years on the date of commission of the offence.

(ii) Though this fact was neither brought to the notice of the Sessions Judge and nor the High Court and was brought to the notice of this Court for the first time by Appellant No. 2 in this appeal, yet in the light of law laid down by this Court in several decisions, Appellant No. 2 was entitled to raise this plea even in this appeal.

(iii) So far as the issue relating to the genuineness of the date of birth of Appellant No. 2 was concerned, firstly, it was not in dispute that Appellant No. 2 had filed his date of birth certificate in the Sessions Court. Secondly, the prosecution did not object to the correctness of the birth certificate before the Sessions Judge. Thirdly, this Court by order granted bail to Appellant No. 2 on this ground observing therein that since he was juvenile at the time of commission of the offence and was below eighteen years, which was not disputed by the Respondent-State and lastly, even at the time of hearing of this appeal, the Respondent-State did not dispute the date of birth certificate of Appellant No. 2.

# SIXTEEN

# STATE OF BIHAR VS. RAJBALLAV PRASAD, 2016

**Hon'ble Judges/Coram:** A.K. Sikri and Abhay Manohar Sapre, JJ.

**Act/ Sections:** Protection of Children from Sexual Offences Act, 2012 - Section 3, Protection of Children from Sexual Offences Act, 2012 - Section 4, Protection of Children from Sexual Offences Act, 2012 - Section 5, Protection of Children from Sexual Offences Act, 2012 - Section 6, Protection of Children from Sexual Offences Act, 2012 - Section 7, Protection of Children from Sexual Offences Act, 2012 - Section 8, Protection of Children from Sexual Offences Act, 2012 - Section 9, Protection of Children from Sexual Offences Act, 2012 - Section 29; Indian Penal Code, 1860 (IPC) - Section 34, Indian Penal Code, 1860 (IPC) - Section 120B, Indian Penal Code, 1860 (IPC) - Section 212, Indian Penal Code, 1860 (IPC) - Section 366A, Indian Penal Code, 1860 (IPC) - Section 370, Indian Penal Code, 1860 (IPC) - Section 370A, Indian Penal Code, 1860 (IPC) - Section 376, Indian Penal Code, 1860 (IPC) - Section 420; Immoral Traffic (Prevention) Act, 1956 - Section 4, Immoral Traffic (Prevention) Act, 1956 - Section 5, Immoral Traffic (Prevention) Act, 1956 - Section 6; Code of Criminal Procedure, 1973 (CrPC) - Section 82, Code of Criminal Procedure, 1973 (CrPC) - Section 83, Code of Criminal Procedure, 1973 (CrPC) - Section 439(2); Constitution of India - Article 136

**No. of pages of the original Judgement: 12**

**Citation:** AIR2017SC630, (2017)2SCC178, MANU/SC/1525/2016

**Case Note**: Criminal - Grant of bail - Validity thereof - Respondent was facing trial, wherein he was charged for committing various offences - Respondent's bail application was dismissed by Trial Court - Respondent preferred another bail petition before High Court - High Court directed release of Respondent on bail - Certain conditions were also imposed while granting bail - Hence, present appeal by State - Whether High Court should not have granted bail to Respondent

**Facts:** The Respondent was facing trial, wherein he was charged for committing offences under Sections 376, 420/34, 366A, 370, 370A, 212, 120B of the Indian Penal Code, 1860, Sections 4, 6 and 8 of the Protection of Children from Sexual Offences Act, 2012 and Sections 4, 5 and 6 of the Immoral Traffic Act, 1956. Pending trial, the Respondent filed bail application which was dismissed by the Trial Court. The Respondent approached the High Court for grant of bail. However, permission was sought to withdraw the said bail application and accepting this request, the bail petition was dismissed as withdrawn. Within three weeks thereafter, the Respondent preferred another bail petition before the High Court. The High Court directed release of the Respondent on bail. Certain conditions were also imposed while granting the bail. Hence, the present appeal by the State.

**Hon'ble Apex Court Held, while allowing the appeal**: (i) It is expected that once the discretion is exercised by the High Court on relevant considerations and bail is granted, this Court would normally not interfere with such a discretion, unless it is found that the discretion itself is exercised on extraneous considerations and/or the relevant factors which need to be considered while exercising such a discretion are ignored or bypassed.

(ii) The Appellant was not seeking cancellation of bail on the ground that the Respondent misconducted himself after the grant of bail or new facts have emerged which warrant cancellation of bail.

(iii) The prosecutrix and her family members made representations claiming that the Respondent was threatening the family members of the prosecutrix. So much so, having regard to several complaints of intimidation of witnesses made on behalf of the prosecutrix and her family members, the State administration has deputed a force for the safety and security of the prosecutrix and her family. In spite of this, the High Court made casual and cryptic remarks that there was no material showing that the accused had interfered with the trial by tampering evidence. The paramount consideration should have been pointed, whether there were any chances of the Accused person fleeing from justice or reasonable apprehension that the Accused person would tamper with the evidence/trial if released on bail. These aspects were not dealt with by the High Court appropriately and with the seriousness they deserved.

(iv) The High Court also ignored another vital aspect, namely, while rejecting the bail application of co-accused, the High Court had ordered expeditious, nay, day-to-day trial to ensure that the trial comes to an end most expeditiously. When order had already been passed to fast-track the trial, and the application for bail by co-accused was also rejected, the High Court, while considering the bail application of the Respondent, was supposed to take into consideration this material fact as well. It was not a fit case for grant of bail to the Respondent at this stage and grave error was committed by the High Court in this behalf.

(v) Few other material witnesses, including father and sister of the prosecutrix, were yet to be examined. As per the records, threats were extended to the prosecutrix as well as her family members. The impugned order passed by the High Court was set aside.

ppp

# SEVENTEEN

## STATE OF GUJARAT AND ORS. VS. NARAYAN, 2021

**Hon'ble Judges/Coram**: Dr. D.Y. Chandrachud and B.V. Nagarathna, JJ.

**Act/ Sections:** Prisons Act, 1894 - Section 59, Section 354, Indian Penal Code, 1860 (IPC) - Section 357, Indian Penal Code, 1860 (IPC) - Section 376(2)

**No. of pages of the original Judgement: 012**

**Citation**: AIR2021SC5096, MANU/SC/0942/2021

**Case Note**: Criminal - Release on furlough - FIRregistered against the Respondent for offences underSections 376(2)(c), 377, 354, 344, 357, 342, 323, 504, 506(2), 120-B, 212, 153 and 114 of the Indian Penal Code 1860 - Charges were framed - Respondent's application for release on furlough rejected by authorities - Single Judge of High Court in Petition challenging rejection allowed Respondent to be released on furlough - Order assailed in present petition - Whether Respondent entitled to be released on furlough?

**Facts:** The present petition came up to challenge the order of release on furlough granted to Respondent. Originally plea of release was rejected by concerned authority. Hence, the present petition.

**Hon'ble Apex Court Held, while allowing the Appeal**: Bombay Furlough and Parole Rules do not confer a legal right on a prisoner to be released on furlough. The use of the expression "may be released" in Rule 3 indicates the absence of an absolute right.

The record does not show that the Respondent has made any efforts to escape from lawful custody. After the grant of furlough in December 2020 and interim bail from 31 January 2021 till 3 February 2021, the Respondent surrendered to the authorities. Thus, Rule 4(10) of the Rules cannot be relied upon to refuse furlough leave to the Respondent. Jail Superintendent has given a negative opinion based on the fact that the Respondent kept a mobile phone inside the jail illegally and attempted to make contacts with the outside world. Rule 4(4) of the Rules provides for denial of furlough on grounds of disturbance to public peace and tranquillity. The order dated 8 May 2021 has adduced a number of circumstances which cumulatively indicate that the release of the Respondent on furlough may lead to a violation of public peace. The order refers specifically to the threat he and his followers pose to the complainant and other persons who deposed at the trial. An attempt has been made to threaten and suborn the investigating team and the witnesses. The Respondent and his father have a mass following of persons who owe loyalty to them and there is a reasonable apprehension of a disruption of public peace and tranquillity. During the trial, attempts have been made to bribe public officials. The conduct after the trial, in jail, has not been shown to be above reproach. The Respondent was released earlier this year to accommodate a genuine need to attend to his mother's health at the relevant time. Based on this, line of reasoning of the High Court not agreeable.

Appeal allowed and the impugned judgment set aside.

ᐅᐅᐅ

# EIGHTEEN

# GANGA PRASAD MAHTO VS. STATE OF BIHAR AND ORS., 2019

**Hon'ble Judges/Coram**: Abhay Manohar Sapre and Dinesh Maheshwari, JJ.

**Act/ Sections**: Indian Penal Code, 1860 (IPC) - Section 376

**No. of pages of the Original Judgement: 03**

**Citation**: (2020)15SCC398, MANU/SC/0409/2019

**Case Note:** Criminal - Conviction - Section 376 of Indian Penal Code, 1860 (IPC) - Present appeal was directed against judgment passed by High Court whereby High Court dismissed appeal filed by Appellant and upheld order of 4th Additional District & Sessions Judge convicting Appellant - Whether two Courts below were justified in convicting Appellant for an offence punishable under Section 376 of IPC.

**Facts:** PW-3 lodged a complaint complaining therein that, Appellant entered into her house when she was alone and threatened her by showing pistol and committed rape on her. Appellant was prosecuted and eventually convicted for an offence punishable under Section 376 of IPC and sentenced to undergo rigorous imprisonment for 7 years by Sessions Judge. Conviction and sentence was upheld by High Court. Appellant (Accused) was now in appeal in present Court against his concurrent conviction/sentence.

**Hon'ble Apex Court Held, while allowing the appeal**: 1. Complainant was not examined by Doctor after alleged incident. Second, in absence of any medical examination done, prosecution did not examine any doctor in trial in support of their case. Similar type of complaints were being made in past by complainant against other persons also and such complaints were later found false. There was enmity between Appellant and husband of prosecutrix, due to which their relations were not cordial. It had also come in evidence that, prosecutrix was in habit of implicating all persons by making wild allegations of such nature against those with whom she or/and her husband were having any kind of disputes. There was no eye witness to alleged incident and one, who was cited as witness, i.e., PW-2 was a chance witness on whose testimony, a charge of rape could not be established. So far as PW-1, husband of complainant, was concerned, he admitted that he was away and returned to village next day morning of incident.

2. Prosecution had failed to prove case of rape alleged by Complainant (PW-3) against the Appellant beyond reasonable doubt. There was no evidence adduced by prosecution to prove commission of offence of rape by Appellant on PW-3 and evidence adduced was not sufficient to prove case of rape against Appellant.

3. Impugned order was set aside. Appellant was acquitted from charges leveled against him. Appeal allowed.

ppp

# NINETEEN

# ANVERSINH VS. STATE OF GUJARAT, 2021

**Hon'ble Judges/Coram:** N.V. Ramana, S. Abdul Nazeer and Surya Kant, JJ.

**Act/ Sections**: Code of Criminal Procedure, 1973 (CrPC) - Section 161, Code of Criminal Procedure, 1973 (CrPC) - Section 313; Indian Contract Act, 1872; Indian Penal Code, 1860 (IPC) - Section 359, Indian Penal Code, 1860 (IPC) - Section 361, Indian Penal Code, 1860 (IPC) - Section 363, Indian Penal Code, 1860 (IPC) - Section 366, Indian Penal Code, 1860 (IPC) - Section 376

**No. of pages of the Original Judgement: 08**

**Citation:** AIR2021SC477, (2021)3SCC12, MANU/SC/0018/2021

**Case Note:** Criminal - Conviction - Consensual affair - Sections 363, 366 and 376 of Indian Penal Code, 1860 - FIR was registered against Appellant accused for offence punishable under Sections 376, 363 and 366 of Code - Additional Sessions Judge held that testimony of prosecutrix unequivocally established that she had been raped three to four times by Appellant, thus meriting his conviction under Section 376 of Code - Trial Court also convicted Appellant for offence under Sections 363 and 366 of Code - On appeal, High Court observed that factum of prosecutrix being in love with Accused having been established beyond any doubt coupled with fact that they used to meet frequently, Appellant could not be held guilty of committing rape under Section 376 of Code - However, there being no evidence suggesting that prosecutrix had consented to be taken from her parents' lawful custody and given her undisputable minority, Appellant's conviction under Sections 363 and 366 of Code was sustained - Hence, present appeal - Whether consensual affair could be defence against charge of kidnapping minor.

**Facts:** The Additional Sessions Judge held that the testimony of the prosecutrix unequivocally established that she had been raped three to four times by the Appellant, thus meriting his conviction under Section 376 of Indian Penal Code. It was further observed that although there was a love affair but considering the fact that the prosecutrix was minor at the time of occurrence, her consent was wholly irrelevant for the charge of kidnapping. In light of the prosecutrix's claim of forcible abduction and discovery along with the Appellant, it was also held that the Appellant had enticed and lured the minor girl with the intention to have intercourse and marriage, and thus all the ingredients of Sections 363 and 366 of Indian Penal Code were well established. The Appellant assailed his conviction before the High Court claiming that the parties were in love owing to which the prosecutrix had left her parents' home and gone with him at her own free will. Additionally, she never raised any protest or alarm despite numerous opportunities to do so and thus none of the constituents of kidnapping' or 'rape was established. The High Court in its order under appeal observed that the factum of the prosecutrix being in love with the Accused having been established beyond any doubt coupled with the fact that they used to meet frequently, the Appellant could not be held guilty of committing rape and his consequential conviction and sentence under Section 376 Indian Penal Code was set aside. However, there being no evidence suggesting that the prosecutrix had consented to be taken from her parents lawful custody and given her undisputable minority, the Appellant's conviction under Sections 363 and 366 of Indian Penal Code was sustained.

**Hon'ble Apex Court Held, while partly allowing the appeal:** (i) The Appellant had unintentionally admitted his culpability. Besides the victim being recovered from his custody, the Appellant admits to having established sexual intercourse and of having an intention to marry her. Although the victim's deposition that she was forcefully removed from the custody of her parents might possibly be a belated improvement but the testimonies of numerous witnesses make out a clear case of enticement. The evidence on record further unequivocally suggests that the Appellant induced the prosecutrix to reach at a designated place to accompany him.

(ii) Behind all the chaff of legalese, the Appellant had failed to propound how the elements of kidnapping had not been made out. His core contention appears to be that in view of consensual affair between them, the prosecutrix joined his company voluntarily. Such a plea, could not be acceded to given the unambiguous language of the statute as the prosecutrix was admittedly below eighteen years of age.

(iii) A bare perusal of the relevant legal provisions, show that consent of the minor is immaterial for purposes of Section 361 of Indian Penal Code. Indeed, as borne out through various other provisions in the Indian Penal Code and other laws like the Indian Contract Act, 1872, minors are deemed incapable of giving lawful consent. Section 361 Indian Penal Code, particularly, goes beyond this simple presumption. It bestows the ability to make crucial decisions regarding a minor's physical safety upon his/her guardians. Therefore, a minor girl's infatuation with her alleged kidnapper cannot by itself be allowed as a defence, for the same would amount to surreptitiously undermining the protective essence of the offence of kidnapping.

(iv) It was apparent that instead of being a valid defence, the Appellant's vociferous arguments were merely a justification which although evokes our sympathy, but can't change the law. Since the relevant provisions of the Indian Penal Code could not be construed in any other manner and a plain and literal meaning thereof leaves no escape route for the Appellant, the Courts below were seemingly right in observing that the consent of the minor would be no defence to a charge of kidnapping. No fault could thus be found with the conviction of the Appellant under Section 366 of Indian Penal Code.

(v) The sentence of five years' rigorous imprisonment awarded by the Courts below, was disproportionate to the facts of the this case. The concerns of both the society and the victim could be respected, and the twin principles of deterrence and correction would be served by reducing the Appellant's sentence to the period of incarceration already undergone by him.

**Ratio Decidendi**: A minor girl's infatuation with her alleged kidnapper cannot by itself be allowed as a defence, for the same would amount to surreptitiously undermining the protective essence of the offence of kidnapping.

ppp

# TWENTY
# RAJA AND ORS. VS. STATE OF KARNATAKA, 2016

**Hon'ble Judges/Coram:** Pinaki Chandra Ghose and Amitava Roy, JJ.

**Act/ Sections**: INDIAN PENAL CODE, 1860 (IPC) - Section 34; INDIAN PENAL CODE, 1860 (IPC) - Section 366; INDIAN PENAL CODE, 1860 (IPC) - Section 376(g); INDIAN PENAL CODE, 1860 (IPC) - Section 392

**No. of pages of the Original Judgement: 10**

**Citation:** AIR2016SC4930, (2016)10SCC506, MANU/SC/1287/2016

**Case Note:** Criminal - Acquittal - Reversal thereof - Sections 34, 366, 376(g) and 392 of Indian Penal Code, 1860 - High Court reversed acquittal of Appellants from charge under Sections 366, 376(g) and 392 read with Section 34 of Indian Penal Code, 1860 as recorded by Trial Court - Hence, present appeal - Whether Prosecution failed to prove charge against Appellants

**Facts**: The Trial Court acquitted the Appellants/Accused of the charges levelled against them. The High Court by the impugned decision reversed the acquittal and the Appellants were convicted under Sections 376(g) and 392 read with Section 34 of Indian Penal Code, 1860. Hence, the present appeal.

**Hon'ble Apex Court Held, while allowing the appeal:** (i) The conduct of Prosecutrix during the alleged ordeal was unlike a victim of forcible rape and betrays somewhat submissive and consensual disposition. From the nature of the exchanges between her and the Accused persons as narrated by her, the same were not at all consistent with those of an unwilling, terrified and anguished victim of forcible intercourse, if judged by the normal human conduct. Her post incident conduct and movements are also noticeably unusual. The medical opinion that she was accustomed to sexual inter course when admittedly she was living separately from her husband for 1 and years before the incident also had its own implication. The medical evidence as such in the attendant facts and circumstances in a way belied the allegation of gang rape.

(ii) The prosecution case, when judged on the touchstone of totality of the facts and circumstances, did not generate the unqualified and unreserved satisfaction indispensably required to enter a finding of guilt against the Appellants. Having regard to the evidence on record as a whole, it was not possible for present Court to unhesitatingly hold that the charge levelled against the Appellants has been proved beyond reasonable doubt. The view taken by the Trial Court was the overwhelmingly possible one. In contrast, the findings of the High Court were decipherably strained in favour of the prosecution by overlooking many irreconcilable inconsistencies, anomalies and omissions rendering the prosecution case unworthy of credit. The High Court exonerated the Appellants of the charge of abduction under Section 366 of Code, 1860, which was an inseverable component of the string of offences alleged against them. The view adopted by the High Court was not a plausible one when juxtaposed to that of the Trial Court. The Appellants were entitled to the benefit of doubt. The impugned judgment and order were set-aside.

ᐅᐅᐅ

# Videos & Tv Shows On Law & Exim

**List of some important videos & TV shows on Law & EXIM by Adv. Jayprakash Somani on his YouTube Channel 'Jayprakash Somani EXIM & Legal'**

**Legal Videos: Hindi -English**

**1)** SLP in Supreme Court / Special Leave Petitions in the Supreme Court of India

**2)** Transfer of Civil & Criminal Cases by the Supreme Court of India / Transfer of Matrimonial Cases

**3)** Appellate Jurisdiction of the Supreme Court of India

**4)** Jurisdictions of the Supreme Court of India

**5)** Public Interest Litigation in the Supreme Court of India / PIL in Supreme Court

**6)** Article 32 Writ Petitions in the Supreme Court of India

**7)** Bail Matters Top 10 Supreme Court Cases

**8)** FIR Quashing in High Court & Supreme Court

**9)** Bail & Anticipatory Bail Matters in Supreme Court

**10)** Insolvency & Bankruptcy Matters in the Supreme Court

**11)** Insolvency & Bankruptcy Code 2016 Part 1

**12)** Insolvency & Bankruptcy Code 2016 Part 2

**13)** Insolvency & Bankruptcy Code 2016 Part 3

**14)** Corporate Liquidation Process

**15)** Supreme Court Rules & Procedures Webinar of 2.5 hour on Zoom

**16)** RDDBFI Act, 1993 (Introduction)

**17)** The Indian Contact Act 1872

**18)** Negotiable Instruments Act (Introduction)

**19)** How to avoid matrimonial disputes& some more videos

**20)** SEBI Matters in the Supreme Court

**21)** Matrimonial Matters: Supreme Court's 20 Case Laws

**22)** Consumer Matters Supreme Court's 20 Case Laws

**23)** Service Matters Supreme Court's 20 Case Laws

**24)** How to Search Lawyer for Your Matter

**25)** Property Matters Supreme Court's 20 Case Laws

**26)** Bail Matters: Supreme Court's 20 Case Laws

**27)** Supreme Court / High Court Vacation Benches

**28)** 69000 Teacher's Recruitment Matters of UP Government in the Supreme Court

**29)** Contempt of Court Matters in the Supreme Court

**30)** Advocate Act's Matters in the Supreme Court

**31)** Business Law Matters in the Supreme Court

**32)** Banking Matters in the Supreme Court

**33)** Labour Law Matters in the Supreme Court

**34)** Arbitration Matters in the Supreme Court

**35)** Careers in Law -Zoom Webinar by Adv. Jayprakash Somani

**36)** Civil Matters in the Supreme Court

**37)** Consumer Protection Act | Consumer Matters in the Supreme Court

**38)** Corporate Matters in the Supreme Court

**39)** Criminal Matters in the Supreme Court

**40)** Role of Respondent in the Supreme Court of India

**41)** Motor Vehicle Accident Matters in Supreme Court with case laws

**42)** Article 131 Original Suits in Supreme Court

**43)** PIL in Supreme Court/ Public Interest Litigations in the Supreme Court of India'

**44)** CAB Citizenship Amendment Bill is not Unconstitutional

**45)** Supreme Court of India Cases & Process – Marathi

**46)** Legal Services Export / Export of Legal Services

**47)** Transfer of Matrimonial Cases by the Supreme Court of India

**48)** Public Interest Litigation PIL

**49)** The Specific Relief Act (Introduction)

**50)** Corporate Insolvency Resolution Process CIRP

**51)** ABMM's Career 5 - Careers in Law

**52)** Transfer of cases by Supreme Court

**53)** Writ Petitions in High Court & Supreme Court of India

**54)** Supreme Court Jurisdictions - Appeals, SLP, Writ Petitions, Transfer, Original, Review, Curative

**55)** LEGAL INDIA TV Show: Cases Handled in Supreme Court

**56)** Corporate Liquidation Process

**57)** Legal Services Export / Export of Legal Services

**58)** Corporate Laws

**59)** Election Matters- Supreme Court's 20 Case Laws

**60)** Companies Act, 2013

**62)** Competition Act, 2002

**63)** Banking Matters - Supreme Court's 20 Case Laws

**64)** Election Matters in the Supreme Court

**65)** Armed Forces Tribunal Matters in the Supreme Court

**66)** Compassionate Appointment Service matter

**67)** Foreign Exchange Management Act FEMA

**68)** Foreign Trade Policy 2021-26 Proposed

**69)** Customs Act 1962

**70)** Narcotic Drugs and Psychotropic Substances Act, 1985 NDPS Act

**71)** Foreign Trade Development & Regulation Act, 1992

**72)** How to Search Good Advocate in the Supreme Court of India

**73)** Sr. Adv Vikas Singh's Interview in Nani Palkhivala Wednesday Law Club

ᕤᕤᕤ

**EXIM Videos: Hindi -English**

**1)** Yes, I can do Import Export Business Easily! 36 points excellent video in Hindi

**2)** Yes, I can do Import Export Business Easily! 36 points excellent video in English

**3)** Import Export Business – Hindi video

**4)** Import Export Business - English video

**5)** Export Import Marathi TV Interview

**6)** Scope for Commerce Students in International Business- TV Show

**7)** Scope for Management Student in International Business- TV Show

**8)** Scope for Engineering Students in International Business – TV Show

**9)** Women in International Business- TV Show

**10)** How to do Import Export Business Successfully!'

**11)** Where one can get full information on Import Export Business?

**12)** What to do import & export?

**13)** Import Export Workshop/ Training/Course/ Diploma

**14)** How to Start Import Export Business & How to grow it. Live Webinar

**15)** Success Stories & Failure Stories in Import & Export Business

**16)** For MSME Scope in Export & Import...

**17)** Exports In Agri. & Food Products – English & some more videos

**18)** Exports to Dubai, Aabudhabii. e. UAE

**19)** Jewellery Exports from India

**20)** How to attend EXIM workshop to become excellent Exporter

**21)** Import Export Best Training Course – Online & Offline

**22)** Agri Product Export

23) Scope for Woman in International Business

24) Management Graduates Scope in International Business

25) Pharma Product's Export

26) Best Import Export Course | Practical Training | Aaronica Global Exim

27) Import Export Business for Commerce Graduates

28) How Do I Get Export Orders? Finding International Buyers

29) What Is APEDA In Import Export Business?

30) Which Is The Best Product To Export From India?

31) EXIM Remark by Manoj Kumar Faridabad

32) EXIM Remarks by Mahesh Telangana

33) What Licenses I Need To Start Import/ Export?

34) How Can I Increase My Import Export Business?

35) Which Is Best B2B Website For Import/Export Business?

36) Export Import Management with Global Marketing

37) How to Start Export Import Business | 51 Points Video

38) Scope for Commerce & Other Graduates in International Business

39) BE A SUCCESSFUL EXPORTER FOR OUR NATION - Marathi video

40) Export of Textile , Cotton, Agri., Food, & other products & services

41) Exports from MP, CG, MH, GJ & CA in Fresh Fruits & Vegetables

42) Exports in Agri. & Food Products- Hindi

43) Start your Online/E-Commerce Business

44) How to Start Export Import Business & Grow it

45) Exports in Textile & Other Products

46) Start and grow EXIM business - Live English Webinar

47)'Import Export Business!' Why, Who, What & How can one do it easily!!

48) Live: Export of Product & Services During & After Lock Down Period

49) Frauds in Import Export Business

50) Import Export for Business Man

51) Import & Export for Women

51) Import & Export for Graduate & Post - Graduate Students

52) Agriculture Exports from India

53) Digital Marketing Setup - Marathi

54) $2^{nd}$ Secret of Successful Businessman

55) Digital Marketing Set up

56) Legal Services Export / Export of Legal Services

57) Export & Import with UAE

**58)** Service Exports / Exports by Service Providers

**59)** Import Export Workshop/ Training/Course/ Diploma

**60)** Exports & Imports with USA

**61)** Selection on Product for Export

**62)** Top Products Exported from India

**63)** What to do import & export?

**64)** ABMM Career 2 - 'Careers in Business & Industries

**65)** How to do Import Export Business Successfully!'

**66)** 5 Secrets of Successful Businessman

**67)** Export from MP, Chhattisgarh & Vidarbha Nagpur

**68)** EXIM Hindi - Textile & Apparel Export

**69)** EXIM Hindi - Export Import Practical Training In Delhi, Kolkata, Mumbai and Pune

**70)** Import Export Business

**71)** Import Export Business Hindi

**72)** Import Export Business English video

**73)** Import Export Business Marathi

**74)** Women in International Business by Exim Guru Adv. Jayprakash Somani

**75)** Opportunities in Foreign Trade- Adv. Jayprakash Somani's special interview

**76)** Textile Exports

**77)** India's Number in Exports. How to improve it?

**78)** 11 Benefits of Exim Workshop

**79)** Export Import Management with Global Marketing- 13 days Training Workshop

**80)** Cosmetic's Export

**82)** Export After COVID

**83)** Spices Exports

**84)** Handicraft Export

**85)** 10 Products India Exports to the World

ppp

# List Of Adv. Jayprakash Somani's Books

1. Supreme Court of India's Leading Case Laws on 'Insolvency & Bankruptcy Code 2016'

2. Bail Matters – Supreme Court's Latest Leading Case Laws

3. Arbitration Matters- Supreme Court's Latest Leading Case Laws

4. Property Matters - Supreme Court's Latest Leading Case Laws

5. Matrimonial Matters- Supreme Court's Latest Leading Case Laws

6. Election Matters- Supreme Court's Latest Leading Case Laws

7.SEBI Matters- Supreme Court's Latest Leading Case Laws

8. Banking Matters- Supreme Court's Latest Leading Case Laws

9. Service Matters- Supreme Court's Latest Leading Case Laws

10. Contempt of Court Matters- Supreme Court's Latest Leading Case Laws

11. Consumer Protection Matters- Supreme Court's Latest Leading Case Laws

12. Corporate Law- Supreme Court's Latest Leading Case Laws

13. Supreme Court's AOR Exam- Leading Cases

14. Armed Force Tribunal - Supreme Court's Latest Leading Case Laws

15. Acquittal From 376 - Supreme Court's Latest Leading Case Laws

16. Negotiable instrument – Supreme Court's Latest Leading Case Laws

17. Contract Act- Supreme Court's Latest Leading Case Laws

18. Insider trading- Supreme Court's Latest Leading Case Laws

19. Foreign Exchange and Management Act- Supreme Court's Latest Leading Case Laws

20. Income Tax Act- Supreme Court's Latest Leading Case Laws

21. Company Law- Supreme Court's Latest Leading Case Laws

22. Competition & Monopoly Matters- Supreme Court's Latest Leading Case Laws

23. Compassionate Appointment- Service Matters- Supreme Court's Latest Leading Case Laws

24. Compulsory Retirement- Service Matters- Supreme Court's Latest Leading Case Laws

25. Voluntary Retirement- Service Matters- Supreme Court's Latest Leading Case Laws

26. Removal/Dismissal/Termination from Service- Supreme Court's Latest Leading Case Laws

27. Seniority- Service Matter- Supreme Court's Latest Leading Case Laws

28. Promotion- Service Matter- Supreme Court's Latest Leading Case Laws

29. Equal Pay for Equal Work- Service Matter- Supreme Court's Latest Leading Case Laws

30. Condition of Service- Service Matter- Supreme Court's Latest Leading Case Laws

31. Customs Act- Supreme Court's Leading Case Laws

32. Information Technology Act- Supreme Court's Leading Case Laws

33. SEC. 125 CR. P. C.- Supreme Court's Leading Case Laws

34. SEC. 498A OF I. P. C.- Supreme Court's Leading Case Laws

35. MOTOR VEHICLE ACT- Supreme Court's Leading Case Laws

36. CONDITION OF SERVICE- SERVICE MATTER- Supreme Court's Leading Case Laws

37. SUSPENSION- SERVICE MATTER- Supreme Court's Leading Case Laws

38. Reservation in SC, ST, OBC- Service Matter- Supreme Court's Leading Case Laws

39. NARCOTIC DRUGS AND PSYCHOTROPIC SUBSTANCES (NDPS) ACT - Supreme Court of India's Latest Leading Case Laws

40. SEC 302 IPC - Supreme Court of India's Latest Leading Case Laws

41. PROTECTION OF CHILDREN FROM SEXUAL OFFENCES ACT (POCSO) - Supreme Court of India's Latest Leading Case Laws

42. PMLA ACT BAIL MATTERS- Supreme Court of India's Leading Case Laws

43. SEC 376 BAIL MATTERS – Supreme Court of India's Leading Case Laws

ೞೞೞ

## Books are available online in India

1. **Notion Press:** https://notionpress.com/author/jayprakash_somani
2. **Amazon:** https://www.amazon.in/s?k=jayprakash+somani
3. **Flipkart:** https://www.flipkart.com/search?q=Jayprakash%20Somani

## Books are available online at International Market

1. **Amazon International:** https://www.amazon.com/

s?k=jayprakash+somani

2. **Amazon United Kingdom:** https://www.amazon.co.uk/s?k=jayprakash+somani

3. **E-Books/Kindle edition at National & International Level:** https://www.amazon.in/s?k=jaypraksh+somani

❧❧❧

www.ingramcontent.com/pod-product-compliance
Lightning Source LLC
Chambersburg PA
CBHW050802160726
48004CB00002B/669